Current
CONTROVERSIES

Police Training and Excessive Force

Other Books in the Current Controversies Series

Police Training and Excessive Force

Pete Schauer, Book Editor

WITHDRAWN FROM
COLLECTION

GREENHAVEN PUBLISHING

Published in 2018 by Greenhaven Publishing, LLC
353 3rd Avenue, Suite 255, New York, NY 10010

Copyright © 2018 by Greenhaven Publishing, LLC

First Edition

Articles in Greenhaven Publishing anthologies are often edited for length to meet page
requirements. In addition, original titles of these works are changed to clearly present
the main thesis and to explicitly indicate the author's opinion. Every effort is made to
ensure that Greenhaven Publishing accurately reflects the original intent of the authors.
Every effort has been made to trace the owners of the copyrighted material.

Cover image: davidkrug/Shutterstock.com

Library of Congress Cataloging-in-Publication Data

Names: Schauer, Peter J., editor.
Title: Police training and excessive force / Pete Schauer, book editor.
Description: New York : Greenhaven Publishing, [2018] | Series: Current
  controversies | Audience: Grade 9 to 12. | Includes bibliographical
  references and index.
Identifiers: LCCN 2017034163| ISBN 9781534502376 (library bound) | ISBN
  9781534502437 (pbk.)
Subjects: LCSH: Police training--Juvenile literature. | Police
  brutality--Juvenile literature.
Classification: LCC HV7923 .P65 2018 | DDC 363.2/32--dc23
LC record available at https://lccn.loc.gov/2017034163

Manufactured in the United States of America

Website: http://greenhavenpublishing.com

Contents

Chapter 1: Is Excessive Force as Common as We Think It Is?

John Whihbey and Leighton Walter Kille

Data indicates that confidence rates in the police are dropping. Some are calling for more transparency—by way of body cameras to record police interactions with citizens.

Yes: Excessive Force Is Extremely Common

Abbie Carver

The police in America are much more likely to use lethal force while on duty than European countries like France, Sweden, and Denmark.

Steven Rosenfeld

Experts say police officers are a brotherhood and will do anything possible to keep their brothers and sisters safe, including covering up and falsifying arrest reports.

Amnesty International

Legal changes need to be made in order to legislate the use of excessive force by police and hold them accountable if they cross the line while on duty.

No: The Prevalance of Excessive Force Is Exaggerated

Alexa Morelli

The strained relationship between the media and the police contributes to how the public perceives police violence.

No: Current Police Training Standards Are Adequate

Foreword

Controversy" is a word that has an undeniably unpleasant connotation. It carries a definite negative charge. Controversy can spoil family gatherings, spread a chill around classroom and campus discussion, inflame public discourse, open raw civic wounds, and lead to the ouster of public officials. We often feel that controversy is almost akin to bad manners, a rude and shocking eruption of that which must not be spoken or thought of in polite, tightly guarded society. To avoid controversy, to quell controversy, is often seen as a public good, a victory for etiquette, perhaps even a moral or ethical imperative.

Yet the studious, deliberate avoidance of controversy is also a whitewashing, a denial, a death threat to democracy. It is a false sterilizing and sanitizing and superficial ordering of the messy, ragged, chaotic, at times ugly processes by which a healthy democracy identifies and confronts challenges, engages in passionate debate about appropriate approaches and solutions, and arrives at something like a consensus and a broadly accepted and supported way forward. Controversy is the megaphone, the speaker's corner, the public square through which the citizenry finds and uses its voice. Controversy is the life's blood of our democracy and absolutely essential to the vibrant health of our society.

Our present age is certainly no stranger to controversy. We are consumed by fierce debates about technology, privacy, political correctness, poverty, violence, crime and policing, guns, immigration, civil and human rights, terrorism, militarism, environmental protection, and gender and racial equality. Loudly competing voices are raised every day, shouting opposing opinions, putting forth competing agendas, and summoning starkly different visions of a utopian or dystopian future. Often these voices attempt to shout the others down; there is precious little listening and considering among the cacophonous din. Yet listening and considering, too, are essential to the health of a democracy. If controversy is democracy's lusty lifeblood, respectful listening and careful thought are its higher faculties, its brain, its conscience.

Current Controversies does not shy away from or attempt to hush the loudly competing voices. It seeks to provide readers with as wide and representative as possible a range of articulate voices on any given controversy of the day, separates each one out to allow it to be heard clearly and fairly, and encourages careful listening to each of these well-crafted, thoughtfully expressed opinions, supplied by some of today's leading academics, thinkers, analysts, politicians, policy makers, economists, activists, change agents, and advocates. Only after listening to a wide range of opinions on an issue, evaluating the strengths and weaknesses of each argument, assessing how well the facts and available evidence mesh with the stated opinions and conclusions, and thoughtfully and critically examining one's own beliefs and conscience can the reader begin to arrive at his or her own conclusions and articulate his or her own stance on the spotlighted controversy.

This process is facilitated and supported in each Current Controversies volume by an introduction and chapter overviews that provide readers with the essential context they need to begin engaging with the spotlighted controversies, with the debates surrounding them, and with their own perhaps shifting or nascent opinions on them. Chapters are organized around several key questions that are answered with diverse opinions representing all points on the political spectrum. In its content, organization, and methodology, readers are encouraged to determine the authors' point of view and purpose, interrogate and analyze the various arguments and their rhetoric and structure, evaluate the arguments' strengths and weaknesses, test their claims against available facts and evidence, judge the validity of the reasoning, and bring into clearer, sharper focus the reader's own beliefs and conclusions and how they may differ from or align with those in the collection or those of classmates.

Research has shown that reading comprehension skills improve dramatically when students are provided with compelling, intriguing, and relevant "discussable" texts. The subject matter of these collections could not be more compelling, intriguing, or urgently relevant to today's students and the world they are poised to inherit. The anthologized articles also provide the basis for stimulating, lively, and passionate classroom debates. Students who are compelled to anticipate objections to their own argument and identify the flaws in those of an opponent read more carefully, think more critically, and steep themselves in relevant context, facts, and information more thoroughly. In short, using discussable text of the kind provided by every single volume in the Current Controversies series encourages close reading, facilitates reading comprehension, fosters research, strengthens critical thinking, and greatly enlivens and energizes classroom discussion and participation. The entire learning process is deepened, extended, and strengthened.

If we are to foster a knowledgeable, responsible, active, and engaged citizenry, we must provide readers with the intellectual, interpretive, and critical-thinking tools and experience necessary to make sense of the world around them and of the all-important debates and arguments that inform it. We must encourage them not to run away from or attempt to quell controversy but to embrace it in a responsible, conscientious, and thoughtful way, to sharpen and strengthen their own informed opinions by listening to and critically analyzing those of others. This series encourages respectful engagement with and analysis of current controversies and competing opinions and fosters a resulting increase in the strength and rigor of one's own opinions and stances. As such, it helps readers assume their rightful place in the public square and provides them with the skills necessary to uphold their awesome responsibility—guaranteeing the continued and future health of a vital, vibrant, and free democracy.

Introduction

> *"The problems arising from the mistreatment of citizens by police officers, commonly termed police brutality, is aggravated by two factors: the tendency of many citizens to exaggerate its extent, and the frequency with which most police officials minimize its significance."*
>
> —*Hubert G. Locke*

Many young children growing up around the world are taught to trust the police, and to always go to a police officer if they are lost or in trouble—but that age-old advice is now questionable, due to the headline-grabbing conflicts police officers have engaged in over the past decade. The training of police officers, and other various officers of the law, has always been subject to examination, but with shootings and killings at the hands of police heavily publicized by the mainstream media, scrutiny has intensified.

Whether that excessive media coverage is deserved or overkill is up for debate, but in this day and age—with social media putting the latest breaking news at everyone's fingertips—it should be expected that events of this nature receive more news coverage, faster. Is it just that increased access to coverage makes it feels as though more citizens are killed by police officers than in the past? Are the numbers really rising—and are a majority of those citizens killed of African American descent?

There is no question that the Black Lives Matter movement has helped shed light on policing and the use of excessive force.

The movement began after the death of seventeen-year-old Trayvon Martin at the hands of George Zimmerman, who was not an officer of the law. From that point on, the movement only became stronger—more widely known following the deaths of Michael Brown in Ferguson, Missouri, and Eric Garner in New York City, with both deaths involving the police. Ultimately, these events have put police training and the use of excessive force under a microscope.

This book takes a look at the controversies surrounding police violence and law enforcement training. Chapter 1 provides an overview of what excessive force is, and then explores if the use of excessive force is as common as it seems to be—analyzing data around the issue, but also looking at how the media can often exploit situations to make them look larger or worse than they may really be. Next, Chapter 2, evaluates whether excessive force is reasonable or warranted in some cases. Are there life-and-death situations where an officer was threatened by a suspect and was forced to take lethal action, or is it never justified to use lethal force? From there, Chapter 3 questions if the use of excessive force has become a larger problem in the current day than it was previously, say in the 1980s. Again, the media comes into play, as we look at whether excessive force really has increased in the last five to ten years, or if media coverage has just become more readily accessible.

Finally, the book concludes with Chapter 4, which raises the ultimate question of if change should be made to the way that police officers are trained—based on all of the data, facts, and analysis revolving around the use of violence in today's police force. Takeaways from *Current Controversies: Police Training and Excessive Force* include learning how police officers are trained, gaining information and statistics on excessive force and when it is justified, and ultimately becoming more educated on how the media portrays the police.

CHAPTER 1

Is Excessive Force as Common as We Think It Is?

Overview: Only Transparency Will Reveal the Truth About Excessive Force

John Whihbey and Leighton Walter Kille

John Whihbey is an assistant professor of Journalism and New Media at Northeastern University in Boston, MA. Leighton Walter Kille is a former assistant arts editor at the Boston Globe *who also serves as a research editor for Journalist's Resource.*

A llegations of the use of excessive force by U.S. police departments continue to generate headlines more than two decades after the 1992 Los Angeles riots brought the issue to mass public attention and spurred some law enforcement reforms. Recent deaths at the hands of police have fueled a lively debate across the nation in recent years.

In a number of closely watched cases involving the deaths of young black men, police have been acquitted, generating uproar and concerns about equal justice for all. On Staten Island, N.Y., the July 2014 death of Eric Garner because of the apparent use of a "chokehold" by an officer sparked outrage. A month later in Ferguson, Mo., the fatal shooting of teenager Michael Brown by officer Darren Wilson ignited protests, and a grand jury's decision not to indict Wilson triggered further unrest. In November, Tamir Rice was shot by police in Cleveland, Ohio. He was 12 years old and playing with a toy pistol. On April 4, 2015, Walter L. Scott was shot by a police officer after a routine traffic stop in North Charleston, S.C. The same month, Freddie Gray died while in police custody in Baltimore, setting off widespread unrest. The policeman in the South Carolina case, Michael T. Slager, was charged with murder based on a cellphone video. In Baltimore, the driver of the police van in which Gray died, Caesar Goodson, was charged with second-degree murder, with lesser charges for five other officers. There have been no indictments in the earlier cases.

These follow other recent incidents and controversies, including an April 2014 finding by the U.S. Department of Justice (DOJ), following a two-year investigation, that the Albuquerque, N.M., police department "engages in a pattern or practice of use of excessive force, including deadly force, in violation of the Fourth Amendment," and a similar DOJ finding in December 2014 with regard to the Cleveland police department. In March 2015, the DOJ also issued a report detailing a pattern of "clear racial disparities" and "discriminatory intent" on the part of the Ferguson, Mo., police department.

As the *Washington Post* reported in July 2015, a pervasive problem that is only now beginning to be recognized is the lack of training for officers dealing with mentally ill persons, a situation that can often escalate to violent confrontations.

The events of 2014-2016 have prompted further calls by some police officials, politicians and scholars for another round of national reforms, in order to better orient "police culture" toward democratic ideals.

Two sides, disparate views

Surveys in recent years with minority groups—Latinos and African Americans, in particular—suggest that confidence in law enforcement is relatively low, and large portions of these communities believe police are likely to use excessive force on suspects. A 2014 Pew Research Center survey confirms stark racial divisions in response to the Ferguson police shooting, as well, while Gallup provides insights on historical patterns of distrust. According to a Pew/*USA Today* poll conducted in August 2014, Americans of all races collectively "give relatively low marks to police departments around the country for holding officers accountable for misconduct, using the appropriate amount of force, and treating racial and ethnic groups equally." Social scientists who have done extensive field research and interviews note the deep sense of mistrust embedded in many communities.

Numerous efforts have been made by members of the law enforcement community to ameliorate these situations, including promising strategies such as "community policing." Still, from a police perspective, law enforcement in the United States continues to be dangerous work—America has a relatively higher homicide rate compared to other developed nations, and has many more guns per capita. Citizens seldom learn of the countless incidents where officers choose to hold fire and display restraint under extreme stress. Some research has shown that even well-trained officers are not consistently able to fire their weapon in time before a suspect holding a gun can raise it and fire first; this makes split-second judgments, even under "ideal" circumstances, exceptionally difficult. But as the FBI points out, police departments and officers sometimes do not handle the aftermath of incidents well in terms of transparency and clarity, even when force was reasonably applied, fueling public confusion and anger.

In 2013, 49,851 officers were assaulted in the line of duty, with an injury rate of 29.2 percent, according to the FBI. Twenty-seven were murdered that year.

FBI Director: No "reliable grasp" of problem

How common are such incidents of police use of force, both lethal and nonlethal, in the United States? Has there been progress in America? The indisputable reality is that we do not fully know. FBI Director James B. Comey stated the following in a remarkable February 2015 speech:

> Not long after riots broke out in Ferguson late last summer, I asked my staff to tell me how many people shot by police were African-American in this country. I wanted to see trends. I wanted to see information. They couldn't give it to me, and it wasn't their fault. Demographic data regarding officer-involved shootings is not consistently reported to us through our Uniform Crime Reporting Program. Because reporting is voluntary, our

data is incomplete and therefore, in the aggregate, unreliable.

I recently listened to a thoughtful big city police chief express his frustration with that lack of reliable data. He said he didn't know whether the Ferguson police shot one person a week, one a year, or one a century, and that in the absence of good data, "all we get are ideological thunderbolts, when what we need are ideological agnostics who use information to try to solve problems." He's right.

The first step to understanding what is really going on in our communities and in our country is to gather more and better data related to those we arrest, those we confront for breaking the law and jeopardizing public safety, and those who confront us. "Data" seems a dry and boring word but, without it, we cannot understand our world and make it better.

How can we address concerns about "use of force," how can we address concerns about officer-involved shootings if we do not have a reliable grasp on the demographics and circumstances of those incidents? We simply must improve the way we collect and analyze data to see the true nature of what's happening in all of our communities.

The FBI tracks and publishes the number of "justifiable homicides" reported by police departments. But, again, reporting by police departments is voluntary and not all departments participate. That means we cannot fully track the number of incidents in which force is used by police, or against police, including non-fatal encounters, which are not reported at all.

Without a doubt, training for police has become more standardized and professionalized in recent decades. A 2008 paper in the *Northwestern University Law Review* provides useful background on the evolving legal and policy history relating to the use of force by police and the "reasonableness" standard by which officers are judged. Related jurisprudence is still being defined, most recently in the 2007 *Scott v. Harris* decision by the U.S. Supreme Court. But inadequate data and reporting—and the challenge of uniformly defining excessive versus justified force—make objective understanding of trends difficult.

A 2015 report conducted for the Justice Department analyzed

394 incidents involving deadly police force in Philadelphia from 2007-2014. It found that "officers do not receive regular, consistent training on the department's deadly force policy"; that early training among recruits is sometimes inadequate in regard to these issues; that investigations into such incidents are not consistent; and that officers "need more less-lethal options."

For perhaps the best overall summary of police use-of-force issues, see "A Multi-method Evaluation of Police Use of Force Outcomes: Final Report to the National Institute of Justice," a 2010 study conducted by some of the nation's leading criminal justice scholars.

Available statistics, background on use of force

The Justice Department releases statistics on this and related issues, although these datasets are only periodically updated: It found that in 2008, among people who had contact with police, "an estimated 1.4% had force used or threatened against them during their most recent contact, which was not statistically different from the percentages in 2002 (1.5%) and 2005 (1.6%)." In terms of the volume of citizen complaints, the Justice Department also found that there were 26,556 complaints lodged in 2002; this translates to "33 complaints per agency and 6.6 complaints per 100 full-time sworn officers." However, "overall rates were higher among large municipal police departments, with 45 complaints per agency, and 9.5 complaints per 100 full-time sworn officers." In 2011, about 62.9 million people had contact with the police.

In terms of the use of lethal force, aggregate statistics on incidents of all types are difficult to obtain from official sources. Some journalists are trying to rectify this; and some data journalists question what few official national statistics are available. The Sunlight Foundation explains some of the data problems, while also highlighting databases maintained by the Centers for Disease Control (CDC). The available data, which does not paint a complete national picture, nevertheless raise serious questions, Sunlight notes:

According to the CDC, in Oklahoma the rate at which black people are killed per capita by law enforcement is greater than anywhere else in the country. That statistic is taken from data collected for the years 1999–2011. During that same time period, Oklahoma's rate for all people killed by law enforcement, including all races, is second only to New Mexico. However, Oklahoma, the District of Columbia, Nevada and Oregon are all tied for the rate at which people are killed. (The CDC treats the District of Columbia as a state when collecting and displaying statistics.) In Missouri, where Mike Brown lived and died, black people are killed by law enforcement twice as frequently as white people. Nationwide, the rate at which black people are killed by law enforcement is 3 times higher than that of white people.

As mentioned, the FBI does publish statistics on "justifiable homicide" by law enforcement officers: The data show that there have been about 400 such incidents nationwide each year. However, FiveThirtyEight, among other journalism outlets, has examined the potential problems with these figures. News investigations suggest that the rates of deadly force usage are far from uniform. For example, Los Angeles saw an increase in such incidents in 2011, while Massachusetts saw more officers firing their weapon over the period 2009–2013.

The academic community has also provided some insights in this area. A 2008 study from Matthew J. Hickman of Seattle University, Alex R. Piquero of the University of Maryland and Joel H. Garner of the Joint Centers for Justice Studies reviewed some of the best studies and data sources available to come up with a more precise national estimate for incidents of nonlethal force. They note that among 36 different studies published since the 1980s, the rates of force asserted vary wildly, from a high of more than 30% to rates in the low single digits. The researchers analyze Police-Public Contact Survey (PPCS) data and Bureau of Justice Statistics Survey of Inmates in Local Jails (SILJ) data and conclude that an estimated 1.7 percent of all contacts result in police threats or use of force, while 20 percent of arrests do.

A 2012 study in the *Criminal Justice Policy Review* analyzed the patterns of behavior of one large police department—more than 1,000 officers—and found that a "small proportion of officers are responsible for a large proportion of force incidents, and that officers who frequently use force differ in important and significant ways from officers who use force less often (or not at all)." A 2007 study in *Criminal Justice and Behavior,* "Police Education, Experience and the Use of Force," found that officers with more experience and education may be less likely to use force, while a review of case studies suggests that specific training programs and accountability structures can lower the use of violence by police departments.

A 2016 working paper from the National Bureau of Economic Research (NBER) came to a conclusion that surprised some observers. Across the U.S., though blacks are 21.3 percent more likely to be involved in an altercation with police where a weapon is drawn, the researchers found no racial differences in police shootings: "Partitioning the data in myriad ways, we find no evidence of racial discrimination in officer-involved shootings. Investigating the intensive margin—the timing of shootings or how many bullets were discharged in the endeavor—there are no detectable racial differences."

Researchers continue to refine analytical procedures in order to make more accurate estimates based on police reports and other data.

Characteristics of suspects

A widely publicized report in October 2014 by ProPublica, a leading investigative and data journalism outlet, concluded that young black males are 21 times more likely to be shot by police than their white counterparts: "The 1,217 deadly police shootings from 2010 to 2012 captured in the federal data show that blacks, age 15 to 19, were killed at a rate of 31.17 per million, while just 1.47 per million white males in that age range died at the hands of police."

Research has definitively established that "racial profiling" by law enforcement exists—that persons of color are more likely to be stopped by police. FBI Director James Comey's 2015 comments are again relevant here:

> [P]olice officers on patrol in our nation's cities often work in environments where a hugely disproportionate percentage of street crime is committed by young men of color. Something happens to people of good will working in that environment. After years of police work, officers often can't help but be influenced by the cynicism they feel.
>
> A mental shortcut becomes almost irresistible and maybe even rational by some lights. The two young black men on one side of the street look like so many others the officer has locked up. Two white men on the other side of the street—even in the same clothes—do not. The officer does not make the same association about the two white guys, whether that officer is white or black. And that drives different behavior. The officer turns toward one side of the street and not the other. We need to come to grips with the fact that this behavior complicates the relationship between police and the communities they serve.

While the cases of Rodney King in 1991 and Amadou Diallo in 1999 heightened the country's awareness of race and policing, research has not uniformly corroborated the contention that minorities are more likely, on average, to be subject to acts of police force than are whites. A 2010 paper published in the *Southwestern Journal of Criminal Justice* reviewed more than a decade's worth of peer-reviewed studies and found that while many studies established a correlation between minority status and police use of force, many other studies did not—and some showed mixed results.

Of note in this research literature is a 2003 paper, "Neighborhood Context and Police Use of Force," that suggests police are more likely to employ force in higher-crime neighborhoods generally, complicating any easy interpretation of race as the decisive factor in explaining police forcefulness. The researchers, William Terrill of Northeastern University and Michael D. Reisig of Michigan State University, found that "officers are significantly more likely to use higher levels of force when encountering criminal suspects in high crime areas and neighborhoods with high levels of concentrated disadvantage independent of suspect behavior and other statistical controls." Terrill and Reisig explore several hypothetical explanations and ultimately conclude:

> Embedded within each of these potential explanations is the influence of key sociodemographic variables such as race, class, gender, and age. As the results show, when these factors are considered at the encounter level, they are significant. However, the race (i.e., minority) effect is mediated by neighborhood context. Perhaps officers do not simply label minority suspects according to what Skolnick (1994) termed "symbolic assailants," as much as they label distressed socioeconomic neighborhoods as potential sources of conflict.

In studying the Seattle and Miami police departments, the authors of the 2010 National Institute of Justice report also conclude that "non-white suspects were less likely to be injured than white suspects ... where suspect race was available as a variable for analysis. Although we cannot speculate as to the cause of this finding, or whether it is merely spurious, it is encouraging that minority suspects were not *more likely* to be injured than whites."

Use of Tasers and other "less lethal" weapons

A 2011 report from the National Institute of Justice, "Police Use of Force, Tasers and Other Less-Lethal Weapons," examines the effectiveness and health outcomes of incidents involving CEDs (conducted energy devices), the most common of which is the Taser. The report finds that: (1) Injury rates vary widely when officers use force in general, ranging from 17% to 64% for citizens and 10% to 20% for officers; (2) Use of Tasers and other CEDs can reduce the statistical rate of injury to suspects and officers who might otherwise be involved in more direct, physical conflict—an analysis of 12 agencies and more than 24,000 use-of-force cases "showed the odds of suspect injury decreased by almost 60% when a CED was used"; and (3) A review of fatal Taser incidents found that many involved multiple uses of the device against the suspect in question.

A 2011 study, "Changes in Officer Use of Force Over Time: A Descriptive Analysis of a National Survey," documents trends in the use of non-lethal force by law enforcement officers (LEAs). The results indicate that CED use has risen significantly (to about 70% of LEAs), while baton use is down to 25% in 2008. "CED use was ranked among the most-used tactics from 2005 to 2008," the scholars conclude. "Excessive-force complaints against LEAs, internally generated, have more than doubled from 2003 to 2008. Officer injuries varied little from 2003 to 2008, but they are still only about half as common as suspect injuries. Also, only 20% of LEAs collect injury data in a database, complicating future research."

Potential impact of body cameras

Video recordings of interactions between the police and the public have increased significantly in recent years as technology has improved and the number of distribution channels has expanded. Any standard smartphone can now make a video—as was the case in the Walter L. Scott shooting—and dash-mounted cameras in police cars have become increasingly common.

The mandatory adoption of body cameras by police has been suggested to increase transparency in interactions between law-enforcement officials and the public. A 2014 study from the U.S. Department of Justice, "Police Officer Body-Worn Cameras: Assessing the Evidence," reviews available research on the costs and benefits of body-worn camera technology. The author, Michael D. White of Arizona State University, identified five empirical studies on body cameras, and assesses their conclusions. In particular, a year after the Rialto, Calif., police department began requiring all officers to wear body cameras, use of force by officers fell by 60% and citizen complaints dropped by nearly 90%. The searcher notes:

> The decline in complaints and use of force may be tied to improved citizen behavior, improved police officer behavior, or a combination of the two. It may also be due to changes in citizen

complaint reporting patterns (rather than a civilizing effect), as there is evidence that citizens are less likely to file frivolous complaints against officers wearing cameras. Available research cannot disentangle these effects; thus, more research is needed.

The studies also noted concerns about the cost of the required devices, training and systems for storing video footage; potential health and safety effects; and especially privacy concerns, both for citizens and the police. In April 2015, a bill being considered in the Michigan State legislature would exempt some body-camera footage from the state's Freedom of Information (FOI) laws. Those who spoke in favor of the law included a conservative Republican legislator and an ACLU representative.

Public opinion and media

The coverage of such incidents by mass media has been studied by researchers, some of whom have concluded that the press has often distorted and helped justify questionable uses of force. Finally, survey data continue to confirm the existence of undercurrents of racism and bias in America, despite demonstrable social progress; a 2014 Stanford study shows how awareness of higher levels of black incarceration can prompt greater support among whites for tougher policing and prison programs.

Excessive Force Runs Rampant in the United States

Abbie Carver

Abbie Carver is a 2017 graduate of the Michigan State University College of Law. She served as associate editor of the International Law Review and was also a teaching assistant for Civil Procedure and for Legal Research and Writing.

This year, allegations of police violence and use of excessive force have generated many disturbing headlines.[1] So far this year, 807 people have been shot and killed by police officers.[2] Although there is no federal database that reports police violence,[3] studies suggest that in 2015, police killed a total of 1,152 people in the U.S.[4] Many of these cases involved questionable deaths of young black men.[5] For example, in August of 2014, teenager Michael Brown was fatally shot by an officer in Ferguson, Missouri.[6] In November 2014, twelve year old Tamir Rice was shot by Cleveland, Ohio police when he was playing with a toy pistol.[7]

Neither police officers in these cases were indicted.[8] In the United States, it is possible for an officer to be sued for an intentional tort; negligence; a violation of the Civil Rights Act - 42 U.S.C. sec. 1983; and be charged under both state and federal criminal codes. Id. However, despite the persistent problem of police officers' excessive use of force, courts continue to avoid second-guessing police actions and only sanction severely egregious misconduct.[9]

American police are 18 times more lethal than Danish police and 100 times more lethal than Finnish police.[10] In addition, American police kill significantly more frequently than police in France, Sweden and other European countries.[11] Paul Hirschfield, a scholar of sociology and criminal justice studied

"Why Do U.S. Police Officers Use More Excessive Force Against Civilians Than Many European Countries and What Can Be Done?," by Abbie Carver, Michigan State University College of Law International Law Review, December 13, 2016. Reprinted by Permission. Abbie Carver, Michigan State International Law Review.

police violence in both Europe and the United States and attempted to identify the root causes of the high rates of police lethality in the U.S.[12] First, Hirschfield suggests that most state laws in the U.S. make it relatively easy for adults to purchase guns; therefore, American police are "primed to expect guns."[13] Unsurprisingly, the study found that American civilians armed with weapons (even non-lethal weapons) were more likely to be killed by police. [14] However, the availability of weapons is not unique to the United States; although knife violence is a persistent problem in England, British police only killed one person wielding a knife in 2008 (who happened to be a hostage-taker).[15] Hirschfield also suggests that pervasive racism in the United States makes civilians more vulnerable to police violence.[16] However, many studies conducted in the U.S. over the past few years have suggested that racism is not the cause of pervasive police violence—that violence equally applies to all American races.[17] Regardless of the cause of fear, these findings suggest that police officers use excessive force when they fear civilians' use of violence.[18]

Hirschfield also found that more than one fourth of deadly force victims in the U.S. were killed in small towns, although only 17 percent of the U.S. population lives in these towns.[19] In Europe, small towns and cities employ municipal police who are generally unarmed and lack arrest authority.[20] In some countries, such as Britain, Ireland, Norway, Iceland and New Zealand, officers are unarmed when they are on patrol.[21] "'The practice is rooted in tradition and the belief that arming the police with guns engenders more gun violence than it prevents."'[22] In contrast, British police officers have considered themselves to be guardians of citizens, who should be easily approachable; 82% of British police do not want to be armed.[23] Hirschfield believes that part of the problem is that the United States fosters police cultures that emphasizes bravery and aggression.[24]

Some activists have argued that gun control laws in the United States should encourage disarmament of both United States citizens and law enforcement, modeled after many European countries.

[25] However, "[m]ost experts agree, however, that it would be counterproductive to suddenly disarm U.S. police officers without addressing the origins of crime."[26]

In the alternative, the United States could adopt a more stringent deadly force standard. In 1989, the United States Supreme Court deemed it constitutionally permissible for police to use deadly force when they reasonably perceive imminent and grave harm. [27] Only 38 American states have laws regulating police and the use of deadly force and almost all of the laws are as permissive as the Supreme Court precedent.[28] In contrast, European countries must conform to the European Convention on Human Rights, which requires all signatories to permit deadly force only when "absolutely necessary" to achieve a lawful purpose.[29] Specific laws in each European country may require additional, more stringent standards; for example, Finland and Norway require police to obtain permission from a superior officer before shooting anyone.[30]

While working towards laws that disarm both citizens and police, the United States may benefit from passing legislation permitting police officers to use deadly force only when absolutely necessary—just as required by the European Convention on Human Rights.

Footnotes

1. John Wihbey & Leighton Walter Kille, Excessive or reasonable force by police? Research on law enforcement and racial conflict, Journalist's Research, http://journalistsresource.org/studies/government/criminal-justice/police-reasonable -force-brutality-race-research-review-statistics (last updated July 28, 2016).

2. Fatal Force, Washington Post, https://www.washingtonpost.com/graphics /national/police-shootings-2016/ (last updated Nov. 6, 2016).

3. Anna Almendrala, Be Wary Of Studies That Deny Racial Bias In Police Shootings, Huffington Post (July 27, 2016), http://www.huffingtonpost.com/entry/police -shootings-studies-racial-bias_us_5796f2d8e4b02d5d5ed2b4aa.

4. 2015 Police Violence Report, Mapping Police Violence, http:// mappingpoliceviolence.org/2015/ (last visited Nov. 6, 2016).

5. Id.

6. Wihbey & Kille, supra note 1.

7. Id.

8. Id.

9. Id.; Jack Ryan, Overview of Police Liability, Legal & Liability Risk Management Institute, http://www.llrmi.com/articles/legal_update/liabilityoverview.shtml (last visited Nov. 6, 2016).

10. Paul Hirschfield, Why American Cops Kill So Many Compared To European Cops, Huffington Post (Nov. 30, 2015), http://www.huffingtonpost.com/entry /american-cops-lethal_us_565cde59e4b079b2818b8870.

11. Id.

12. Id.

13. Id.

14. Id.

15. Id.

16. Id.

17. See id.

18. See id.

19. Id.

20. Id.

21. Rick Noack, 5 countries where most police officers do not carry firearms — and it works well, Washington Post (July 8, 2016), https://www.washingtonpost.com/ news/worldviews/wp/2015/02/18/5-countries-where-police-officers-do-not-carry- firearms-and-it-works-well/.

22. Id.

23. Id.

24. Hirschfield, supra note 8.

25. Noack, supra note 17.

26. Id.

27. Hirschfield, supra note 8

28. Id.

29. Id.

30. Id.

Police Officers Who Use Excessive Force Aren't Disciplined

Steven Rosenfeld

Steven Rosenfeld is the author of multiple books on elections and covers national political issues for AlterNet.

Handcuffed teenagers beaten bloody with guns. Unarmed people shot and killed in their cars. Cops firing guns carelessly into busy streets. Mentally ill people tasered in ambulances. Supervisors refusing to challenge a brutal status quo.

These examples didn't come from the New York City Police Department or Ferguson, Missouri, where the killing of unarmed black men by white cops has created a national outcry over institutional racism and excessive force. They were from Ohio, where the U.S. Department of Justice just finished an investigation and report on abusive and often unconstitutional policing by Cleveland Division of Police between 2010 and 2013. They were compiled before November 22, when a rookie officer shot and killed a 12-year-old African-American boy, Tamir Rice, for waving a toy gun around on a playground.

The DOJ's findings raise big questions. It's not just how widespread is the problem of excessive force and a corresponding lack of accountability. The harder questions include what can be done to change police culture, reverse many out-of-control tactics, and instill a belief across entire forces that restraint and accountability protect cops and civilians.

"We found that field supervisors are failing in some of the most fundamental aspects of their responsibilities—reviewing and investigating the uses of force of the officers under their command, and correcting dangerous tactical choices that place

"15 Reasons America's Police Are So Brutal," by Steven Rosenfeld, Alternet, December 06, 2014. Reprinted by Permission.

the officer and others at risk," Mayor Frank Jackson said of the report, underscoring systemic problems.

When releasing the report, U.S. Attorney General Eric Holder announced the DOJ would work with Cleveland under a consent decree and a federal court will oversee reforms. But a decade ago, the DOJ also investigated police abuses in Cleveland and found similar patterns surrounding excessive force. The city's police pledged reforms would come—yet the department's nasty status quo obviously has resurfaced.

"The voluntary reforms undertaken at that time did not create the systems of accountability necessary to ensure a long-term remedy to these issues," the DOJ's new report said. "More work is necessary to ensure that officers have the proper guidance, training, support, supervision, and oversight to carry out their law enforcement responsibilities safely and in accordance with individuals' constitutional rights."

That summation describing needed reforms typifies today's political rhetoric surrounding the crisis in militarized American policing. The DOJ report didn't say what explicit steps needed to be taken. But it did describe how deeply embedded excessive force was among Cleveland's police, what was wrong and broken in their culture and police procedures, and what was missing and needed to change.

That unvarnished look reveals how hard it will be to reform out-of-control departments, whether in Cleveland, Staten Island, Ferguson, or elsewhere. Here are 15 excerpts from the DOJ's Cleveland report showing how deeply embedded police brutality is, and why recent political rhetoric promising solutions barely scratches the surface.

1. The Street Cops Are On Their Own: "We found that CDP officers too often use unnecessary and unreasonable force in violation of the Constitution. Supervisors tolerate this behavior and, in some cases, endorse it. Officers report that they receive little supervision, guidance, and support from the Division, essentially leaving them to determine for themselves how to perform their difficult and dangerous jobs."

2. Excessive Force Is Expected and Covered Up: "These incidents of excessive force are rooted in common structural deficiencies. CDP's pattern or practice of excessive force is both reflected by and stems from its failure to adequately review and investigate officers' uses of force; fully and objectively investigate all allegations of misconduct; identify and respond to patterns of at-risk behavior; provide its officers with the support, training, supervision, and equipment needed to allow them to do their jobs safely and effectively; adopt and enforce appropriate policies; and implement effective community policing strategies at all levels of CDP."

3. Using Maximum Force Has Become Routine: "For example, we found incidents of CDP officers firing their guns at people who do not pose an immediate threat of death or serious bodily injury to officers or others and using guns in a careless and dangerous manner, including hitting people on the head with their guns, in circumstances where deadly force is not justified. Officers also use less lethal force that is significantly out of proportion to the resistance encountered and officers too often escalate incidents with citizens instead of using effective and accepted tactics to de-escalate tension.

"We reviewed incidents where officers used Tasers, oleoresin capsicum spray ("OC Spray"), or punched people who were already subdued, including people in handcuffs. Many of these people could have been controlled with a lesser application of force. At times, this force appears to have been applied as punishment for the person's earlier verbal or physical resistance to an officer's command, and is not based on a current threat posed by the person. This retaliatory use of force is not legally justified. Our review also revealed that officers use excessive force against individuals who are in mental health crisis or who may be unable to understand or comply with officers' commands, including when the individual is not suspected of having committed any crime at all."

4. Police Don't Know How To De-escalate: Officers "too often fire their weapons in a manner and in circumstances that place innocent bystanders in danger; and accidentally fire them, sometimes fortuitously hitting nothing and other times shooting people and seriously injuring them. CDP officers too often use dangerous and poor tactics to try to gain control of suspects, which results in the application of additional force or places others in danger. Critically, officers do not make effective use of de-escalation techniques, too often instead escalating encounters and employing force when it may not be needed and could be avoided."

5. Top Cops Don't Want To Hear About It: "Force incidents often are not properly reported, documented, investigated, or addressed with corrective measures. Supervisors throughout the chain of command endorse questionable and sometimes unlawful conduct by officers. We reviewed supervisory investigations of officers' use of force that appear to be designed from the outset to justify the officers' actions. Deeply troubling to us was that some of the specially-trained investigators who are charged with conducting unbiased reviews of officers' use of deadly force admitted to us that they conduct their investigations with the goal of casting the accused officer in the most positive light."

6. Top Cops Will Ignore Worst Abuses: "Many of the investigators in CDP's Internal Affairs Unit advised us that they will only find that an officer violated Division policy if the evidence against the officer proves, beyond a reasonable doubt, that an officer engaged in misconduct—an unreasonably high standard reserved for criminal prosecutions and inappropriate in this context. This standard apparently has been applied, formally or informally, for years."

7. Most Cops Face No Disciplinary Threats: "Discipline is so rare that no more than 51 officers out of a sworn force of 1,500 were disciplined in any fashion in connection with a use of force incident over a three-and-a half-year period. However, when we examined CDP's discipline numbers further, it was apparent that in most of those 51 cases the actual discipline imposed was for procedural violations such as failing to file a report, charges were dismissed or deemed unfounded, or the disciplinary process was suspended due to pending civil claims. A finding of excessive force by CDP's internal disciplinary system is exceedingly rare."

8. The DOJ Found These Problems Before. "CDP's systemic failures are such that the Division is not able to timely, properly, and effectively determine how much force its officers are using, and under what circumstances, whether the force was reasonable and if not, what discipline, change in policy or training or other action is appropriate. The current pattern or practice of constitutional violations is even more troubling because we identified many of these structural deficiencies more than ten years ago during our previous investigation of CDP's use of force."

9. Police View Their Beats as War Zones: "Instead of working with Cleveland's communities to understand their needs and concerns and to set crime-fighting priorities and strategies consistent with those needs, CDP too often polices in a way that contributes to community distrust and a lack of respect for officers—even the many officers who are doing their jobs effectively. For example, we observed a large sign hanging in the vehicle bay of a district station identifying it as a "forward operating base," a military term for a small, secured outpost used to support tactical operations in a war zone. This characterization reinforces the view held by some—both inside and outside the Division—that CDP is an occupying force."

10. Harassment, Unprovoked Searches Routine: "Some CDP officers violate individuals' Fourth Amendment rights by subjecting them to stops, frisks, and full searches without the requisite level of suspicion. Individuals were detained on suspicion of having committed a crime, with no articulation or an inadequate articulation in CDP's own records of the basis for the officer's suspicion. Individuals were searched "for officer safety" without any articulation of a reason to fear for officer safety. Where bases for detentions and searches were articulated, officers used canned or boilerplate language. Supervisors routinely approved these inadequate reports."

11. Using Tasers Routine and Never Questioned: "The [Cleveland] Plain Dealer [newspaper] also reported that, between October 2005 and March 2011, CDP officers used Tasers 969 times, all but five of which the Division deemed justified and appropriate (a 99.5% clearance rate which one police expert said "strains credibility"). The Plain Dealer analyzed similar CDP force data in 2007 and found that supervisors reviewed 4,427 uses of force over four years and justified the force in every single case."

12. The CDP Stonewalled DOJ Investigators: "We note that CDP's inability to produce key documents raises serious concerns regarding deficiencies in the Division's systems for tracking and reviewing use of force and accountability-related documents… CDP did not, for example, produce deadly force investigations that occurred after April of 2013 despite multiple requests. CDP was not able to produce some 2012 use of less lethal force reports until more than a year after our initial request for documents and failed to provide a justification for this delay."

13. CDP Didn't Want to Be Accountable: "CDP's inability to track the location of critical force-related documents is itself evidence of fundamental breakdowns in its systems and suggests that any internal analysis or calculation of CDP's use of force is likely incomplete and inaccurate. It also suggests that CDP does not accept that they are accountable for documenting and explaining their decisions in such matters to civilian leadership, the City, and the community as a whole."

14. Arrest Reports Cover Up Use Of Force: "Our review of a sample of 2012 arrest records for persons charged with resisting arrest suggests that some uses of force are not being reported. For the months of February, June and August 2012, there were 111 resisting arrest incidents, and for seven of these—over six percent—CDP acknowledges that no use of force report can be located… The inability to produce Taser firing histories compounds our concerns about the reliability of the data and undermines the assertion that Taser uses have declined."

15. There Are No Clear Policies on Using Force. "Police departments must ensure appropriate training in how and when to use force, and provide the supervision necessary for sufficient oversight of officers' use of force. Departments must also provide their officers clear, consistent policies on when and how to use and report force. Departments must implement systems to ensure that force is consistently reported and investigated thoroughly and fairly, using consistent standards…

"CDP fails in all of these areas, and this has created an environment that permits constitutional violations. It has also created an atmosphere within CDP in which there is little confidence in the fairness of the disciplinary process—a lack of confidence which extends from the rank and file all the way to the highest levels of the Division and City leadership."

No Quick or Easy Solutions

The DOJ report on excessive force by Cleveland's police is very revealing. It shows how deeply embedded the culture of abusive policing is, how resistant police departments are to changing, and how the problem is not just what weapons are used by police, but how many officers want to operate with impunity and a military mindset.

These aren't the conclusions of community activists protesting about police brutality and the institutional racism of white officers shooting unarmed black men. These conclusions come from the highest-ranking federal law enforcement officials, who had to use their political power to force the Cleveland Department to open up its records and files.

The DOJ's observation that many of the same problems of excessive force are back more than 10 years after a similar federal investigation and settlement suggests that reforming America's runaway police departments is going to be incredibly difficult. Despite public protests, there's little evidence that police themselves want to change from within.

The Police Need to Be Held Accountable

Amnesty International

Founded in 1961, Amnesty International is a nongovernmental organization that focuses on human rights around the world.

Hundreds of men and women are killed by police each and every year across the United States. No-one knows exactly how many because the United States does not count how many lives are lost. The limited information available however suggests that African American men are disproportionately impacted by police use of lethal force. While the majority of the unarmed African Americans killed by police officers are men, many African American women have also lost their lives to police violence. Police officers are responsible for upholding the law, as well as respecting and protecting the lives of all members of society. Their jobs are difficult and often dangerous. However, the shooting of Michael Brown in Ferguson, Missouri and countless others across the United States has highlighted a widespread pattern of racially discriminatory treatment by law enforcement officers and an alarming use of lethal force nationwide.

Indeed, just 10 days after Michael Brown was fatally shot in Ferguson, Missouri, on August 9, 2014, St. Louis police officers shot and killed a young black man, Kajieme Powell, 25, who was reportedly holding a knife. Police claims that he was brandishing a knife were not borne out by the available video footage of the shooting. Some of the individuals killed by police in the United States include the following: Rekia Boyd, an unarmed 22-year-old black woman was shot and killed by a Chicago police officer on March 21, 2012; Eric Garner, a 43-year-old black man, died after being placed in a chokehold by New York Police Department officers after being approached by an officer who attempted to arrest

"Deadly Force: Police Use of Lethal Force in the United States," Amnesty International, June 18, 2015. Reprinted by Permission.

him for selling loose, untaxed cigarettes on July 17, 2014; Ezell Ford, 25, an unarmed black man with a history of mental illness, was shot and killed by Los Angeles police officers on August 11 2014; Tamir Rice, a 12-year-old black boy, was shot and killed by officers in Cleveland, Ohio while playing in a park with a toy gun on November 22, 2014; Walter Scott, a 50-year-old unarmed black man, was fatally shot in the back after a traffic stop for a broken light on his car in North Charleston, South Carolina on April 4, 2015; and Freddie Grey, a 25-year-old black man, died from a spinal injury after being taken into police custody in Baltimore, Maryland, on April 19, 2015. These are all cases that have received national media attention; however, there are many more including Hispanic and Indigenous individuals from communities across the country who have died at the hands of the police.

The use of lethal force by law enforcement officers raises serious human rights concerns, including in regard to the right to life, the right to security of the person, the right to freedom from discrimination and the right to equal protection of the law. The United States has a legal obligation to respect, protect and fulfill these human rights and has ratified the International Covenant on Civil and Political Rights and the International Convention on the Elimination of All Forms of Racial Discrimination, which explicitly protects these rights.

One of a state's most fundamental duties which police officers, as agents of the state, must comply with in carrying out their law enforcement duties, is to protect life. In pursuing ordinary law enforcement operations, using force that may cost the life of a person cannot be justified. International law only allows police officers to use lethal force as a last resort in order to protect themselves or others from death or serious injury. The United Nations (UN) Basic Principles on the Use of Force and Firearms provide that law enforcement officials shall not use firearms against persons except in self-defence or the defence of others against the imminent threat of death or serious injury, and that, in any event, "intentional lethal use of firearms may only be made when strictly unavoidable in order to protect life." Furthermore, international law enforcement standards require that force of any kind may be used only when there are no other means available that are likely to achieve the legitimate objective. If the force is unavoidable it must be no more than is necessary and proportionate to achieve the objective, and law enforcement must use it in a manner designed to minimise damage or injury, must respect and preserve human life and ensure medical aid are provided as soon as possible to those injured or affected.

> "States are required to respect and to protect the right to life… The police in any society will at some point be confronted with a situation where they have to decide whether to use force and, if so, how much. Enacting an adequate domestic legal framework for such use of force by police officials is thus a State obligation, and States that do not do this are in violation of their international obligations."
>
> – UN Special Rapporteur on extrajudicial, summary or arbitrary executions

The first step to securing the right to life, according to the UN Special Rapporteur on extrajudicial, summary or arbitrary executions, is the establishment of an appropriate legal framework for the use of force by the police, which sets out the conditions under which force may be used in the name of the State and ensuring a system of responsibility where these limits are transgressed. Furthermore, the UN Special Rapporteur notes that, "The specific relevance of domestic law in this context stems from the fact that the laws of each State remain the first line and in many cases effectively the last line of defence for the protection of the right to life, given the irreversibility of its violation. National and local laws play an important role in defining the understanding by law enforcement officials and the population alike of the extent of the police powers, and the conditions for accountability. As such, there is a strong need to ensure that domestic laws worldwide comply with international standards. It is too late to attend to this when tensions arise."

Amnesty International reviewed US state laws—where they exist—governing the use of lethal force by law enforcement officials and found that they all fail to comply with international law and standards. Many of them do not even meet the less stringent standard set by US constitutional law. Some state laws currently allow for use of lethal force to "suppress opposition to an arrest"; to arrest someone for a "suspected felony"; to "suppress a riot or mutiny"; or for certain crimes such as burglary. A number of statutes allow officers to use lethal force to prevent an escape from a prison or jail. Others allow private citizens to use lethal force if they are carrying out law enforcement activities. Amnesty International found that:

- All 50 states and Washington, DC, fail to comply with international law and standards on the use of lethal force by law enforcement officers;
- Nine states and Washington, DC, currently have no laws on use of lethal force by law enforcement officers; and
- Thirteen states have laws that do not even comply with the lower standards set by US constitutional law on use of lethal force by law enforcement officers.

Many of the nationwide protests in the wake of recent police killings have demanded accountability and international law requires it. All cases of police use of lethal force must be subject to an independent, impartial and transparent investigation and if the evidence indicates that the killing was unlawful, the police officer responsible should be criminally prosecuted. However, accountability for police use of lethal force is severely lacking in the United States. The officer's own police agency usually conducts the investigation before handing the case over to the local prosecutor for review, who, depending on the jurisdiction, either convenes a grand jury or decides directly whether to file charges against the officer. The fact that investigations are handled internally and that prosecutors have to maintain good working relationships with the police as well as fulfill their duty to investigate and prosecute police use of lethal force, has led to calls being made for independent investigations and prosecutors. While this report only examines whether specific accountability measures are provided for in a state's use of lethal force statute, Amnesty International has previously documented concerns with oversight mechanisms in the United States and the need for independent and effective oversight bodies to be established.

Another concern related to accountability is the overly broad statutes governing the use of force, in particular the use of lethal force: If the facts of the case established during an investigation indicate that police used lethal force despite officers having other – less harmful – options at hand to counter a threat or that there was no threat to the life of officers or members of the public at all, this would have to be considered as a violation of international human rights law and standards and – in cases where it has resulted in death – an arbitrary deprivation of life under international law. However, if statutes allow for a use of lethal force below the threshold and outside the strict criteria established by international law, then such statutes actually prevent holding law enforcement officials accountable for violations of human rights.

The majority of deaths at the hands of police are the result of an officer using a firearm. The pervasiveness of firearms among the general population in the US means that officers have to be prepared for the worst when confronting a suspect. An unexpected movement can be mistaken as someone reaching for a firearm even if the suspect is unarmed. However, any use of a firearm – i.e. a weapon designed to kill – by law enforcement must be regulated by specific provisions of the law, establishing a more specific set of rules than for other forms of use of force, and should only be authorized when there is no other way of protecting against a serious threat of death or serious injury.

A key concern in recent cases involving firearms has been the number of shots fired by officers. Michael Brown, for instance, was shot six times, and Kajieme Powell was shot nine times. The firing of so many shots in an urban environment would often be reckless and puts bystanders at risk, and indicates an intentional lethal use of a firearm which under international law and standards may only ever be employed when strictly unavoidable to protect life.

There are a wide range of "less lethal" weapons and other tools available for use in law enforcement which carry less risk of death and injury than that inherent in police use of firearms. However, it should also be recognized that these so-called "less lethal" weapons can also result in serious injury and sometimes death. For example, at least 540 people in the United States died after being shocked with Tasers from 2001 through 2012. Also, even without the use of weapons, as recent cases have demonstrated, chokeholds or other forms of physical force can also be deadly. As such, any other type of force that implies likelihood or high risk of death must also be subject to the same strict restrictions and only be allowed for the purpose of preventing death or serious injury.

While this report focuses on the use of lethal force by law enforcement officers in the United States – that is, principally the use of firearms – an overall change in approach to all aspects of use of force by law enforcement is needed, as at present, police consider use of force to be a normal part of policing operations rather than the exception. International standards clearly require that force should not be used by law enforcement officials unless there are no other means available that are likely to achieve the legitimate objective. If the use of force is unavoidable, it must be the minimum amount of force necessary to achieve the objective, and the use of lethal force should only be used as a last resort; if the use of force is unavoidable, they should minimize damage and injury and ensure those affected receive prompt medical and other assistance. International standards also emphasize the need for law enforcement to use other means before resorting to the use of force, and to be trained in alternatives to the use of force, including the peaceful settlement of conflicts, understanding of crowd behavior, and skills of persuasion, negotiation and mediation.

What is urgently needed is a nationwide review and reform of existing laws, policies, training and practices on police use of lethal force, as well as a thorough review and reform of oversight and accountability mechanisms. As this demonstrates, one of the steps that needs to be taken is for state laws to be thoroughly reformed or, in some cases, replaced with new laws to ensure that police are not permitted to use lethal force except where it is necessary to protect against an imminent threat of death or serious injury.

The Media Fuels Antipolice Sentiment

Alexa Morelli

Writer Alexa Morelli has written for the Odyssey Group and PoliceOne.com. She studied journalism and sports management at the University of Arizona.

Over the past few years, a lot has been happening in our country. We have a new terrorist organization that is influencing our own citizens to commit armed jihad right here on American soil and race relations are worse than they've been since the civil rights movement of the 50s and 60s. Then we have Donald Trump, a billionaire businessman, and reality TV star is currently leading in the Republican primary polls for the 2016 GOP presidential candidate. These are just a few of the significant changes in American culture.

The way America's citizens view law enforcement has also changed. There have always been people who feel disdain towards police officers and their profession (queue N.W.A.s hit song "F*** the Police," originally released in 1988). But today it seems that the publics distrust of police officers has spread far and wide. Many people wonder why that is. There seems to be a significant number of people who blame law enforcements use of heavy-handed tactics combined with cries of racism when it comes to everything from traffic stops to arrests to incarceration. So why has this not been brought to the attention of the general public until somewhat recently? Why are there entire protests, sit-ins and hunger strikes being dedicated to this issue so suddenly? Why are good police officers now being accused of crimes just for doing their jobs? There is a relatively simple answer to these questions.

The culprit to blame for the American people's negative view of police officers is the media.

"The Media's War on Police Officers," by Alexa Morelli, Odyssey Media Group, Inc, December 24, 2015. Reprinted by Permission.

This analysis will consist of three parts. First, a general analysis of the relationship between the media and law enforcement and how they affect each other is necessary. Secondly, a discussion on how the media has changed the way it reports on crime and justice in recent years and examples of this. Finally, how the changes the media has made in the way they report about law enforcement officers and their activity have changed the way Americans view and treat police officers.

The problem with blaming the media for this is that media is a very broad term. The media that this analysis refers to is mostly the mainstream media. Its the big news stations, CNN, NBC, ABC and Fox News. Its the newspapers like the *New York Times*, *Washington Post*, *Chicago Tribune*, and so on. Its journalists in general. It is people that the public trusts and that they have a long-standing relationship with. When it comes to reporting on a police officers violence or misconduct, the reporters often make the races of the police officer and the victim an important part of their story. They bury important facts about the actual cases and they fail to remain objective. If Americans could hear what happened, stating purely the facts of the case while leaving race and opinion out of it, they would be more likely to have a different opinion about the situation, or, at least, be able to form their opinion without the influence of the media. But reporters do not do this. This relates back to Rawls's Justice Theory. If the reporters were being fair and doing their job the way they are supposed to, they would use Rawls's Veil of Ignorance. If the mainstream media did this, things might be different.

The relationship between law enforcement and the media is an important one because they depend on each other.

Crime, justice, and the media have to be studied together because they are inseparable, wedded to each other in a forced marriage where they cohabitate in a fascinating, if raucous relationship, Ray Surette wrote in his novel, *Media, Crime and Criminal Justice*.

The media and crime and justice have this type of dependent relationship because crime and justice are a large percentage of what the media is reporting on. This doesn't always have to do with police officers, but cops play an important role in American society, therefore, they must play an important role in American media and journalism. Because of this, the media can directly affect law enforcement, and they do so by being able to shape the attitudes that people have towards them.

Scholars have long noted the importance of the media in shaping citizens attitudes about crime and justice Kathleen Donovan reported. Many studies have been done on this, making it hard for anyone to argue against.

Furthermore, reporters have changed the way they talk about police officers. They bring more attention than ever to anything negative done by someone in the law enforcement profession while leaving positive stories out of the line-up. CNN contributor, Eliott McLaughlin is one of these reporters. In his article entitled "We're not seeing more police shootings, just more news coverage," he tries to give police officers a bad name. He says that police have been killing innocent black people for years and it is now finally being brought to the nation's attention. But he has no facts or statistics to back this up. In fact, his only source is Robert Bogle, the president and CEO of the *Philadelphia Tribune*, an African American newspaper. He does not interview anyone in the law enforcement profession or anyone with an opinion different than his own. But he does make an important point.

The headlines make it feel as if the country is experiencing an unprecedented wave of police violence, but experts say that isn't the case," McLaughlin said. "Were just seeing more mainstream media coverage.

This is important because it shows that whether someone likes the police or not, everyone can agree that police violence is being brought to our attention more than ever before. Journalists like McLaughlin have started what some people call a hate campaign against police officers.

The seeds of this hate campaign were planted as early as 2009, when, without caring about the facts, President Obama publicly lashed out against a white police officer for arresting Professor Henry Louis Gates, a black Harvard professor. This officer did nothing wrong, Nolte said.

While bringing up how President Obama has influenced the start of this hate campaign brings forward an entirely different topic to analyze, this instance is important because the president went after this police officer for simply doing his job. The police officer was responding to a 9-1-1 call made about the residence. He arrested Gates, even though he was innocent because this is something police officers do all the time. Police officers do this because it is in their job description. It is not their job to arrest the guilty, only a court can determine that. It is their job to arrest possible suspects. The public's view of police officers only got worse after this controversy.

Things were ratcheted up a notch in early 2012 after George Zimmerman, a Florida community watchman, shot and killed Trayvon Martin, Nolte said.

Things took off from there. Suddenly the media was reporting on police officers and how they were racist because of the way the media reported on this case. Many Americans blame the police for Zimmerman being found not guilty even though the police are not the ones who determined this, a jury did. Heather Mac Donald, the Thomas W. Smith fellow at the Manhattan Institute for Policy Research, a public policy think tank in New York City, testified on criminal justice and the deincarceration movement earlier this year.

Mac Donald is also a writer for *City Journal*, and had this to say in her testimony, "The most poisonous claim in the dominant narrative is that our criminal justice system is a product and a source of racial inequity."

The problem with the media calling police officers racists is that the American people are starting to believe that police officers actively seek out black people to arrest or harass them. But, Mac Donald reported prison statistics that there has actually been an increase in white people imprisoned in the last few years, not black people. According to police reports and FBI data, of the roughly 800 people killed by a police officer this year, half were white, and only a quarter were black. This data proves that although the media makes it seem like cops are only shooting unarmed black people, this is not the case. Ninety-five percent of those people killed were for justifiable reasons while only five percent were either undetermined or have the possibility of being because of an illegal action taken by the officer. The media has chosen to either not report on this data at all or bury it beneath the few stories about police injustices. Other than changing the way they report on police officers, the media has made a few other changes due to the rise of citizen journalists and the popularity of social media.

Social media is a topic for a whole other analysis on this subject, but it cannot be left out of this discussion and neither can people who use social media forums to be a new kind of journalist that America has never had before. Because journalism is not a cut and dry profession such as being a doctor or lawyer, really anyone can claim to be a journalist without a certificate or degree. It's very easy for people to start a blog or make a Facebook page or Twitter profile about something they are passionate about and present it to people as truth. It does not matter if they have anyone or anything to back up their claims because, in this day and age, Americans will believe a lot of what they read on the internet. It sounds outrageous to some people, but it is true. Because these people are not actual professionals working for an organization, they set their own ethical guidelines.

This brings forth a whole new set of problems because a lot of these citizen journalists have joined the hate movement of police officers and post anything online to support their claims that police officers are racist and unethical. An even bigger problem brought on by this is that sometimes the mainstream media chooses to interview these people or quote them in their reporting as a source. Because a lot of citizen journalists don't fact check and the mainstream media doesn't take the time to fact check what they are saying, many Americans choose to believe them and their false claims. And the biggest problem of all, the reason this analysis is so important, is the fact that the American people are using this information and acting on it.

Its not easy to prove that the media has changed American's thoughts about police officers because thoughts are much less concrete than actions. But negative thoughts lead to negative actions.

According to the FBI, the number of police officers killed in the line of duty nearly doubled from 27 to 51 between 2013 and 2014. That is nearly one murdered police officer a week during 2014, which was also a little over a year after the mainstream media began its coordinated hate campaigns to demonize America's law enforcement officers, Nolte reports.

This statistic provides a look at the negative affects the media's new way of reporting about law enforcement has had. The number of police officers killed in the line of duty was steadily declining for years. The only variable factor in the last few years has been the media's emphasis on reporting on cases like the Zimmerman case, Ferguson, Brown and so on—cases where police officers either did their job correctly and were not charged rightly so, or were charged because they were an unethical cop and person. This has given cops a bad name overall and has made them less likely to do their job efficiently and stay safe while they do it.

To conclude, it is important to analyze whether or not there is a solution to this madness. In McLaughlin's interview with Bogle, Bogle suggested a solution, video. Many police officers are now being required to wear video cameras on their person so that they have evidence of whether or not they used proper tactics.

Body-worn cameras hold tremendous promise for enhancing transparency, promoting accountability, and advancing public safety for law enforcement officers and the communities they serve," Attorney General Loretta Lynch told MSNBC writer, Will Femia.

In addition to this, black protest groups are encouraging Americans to use their camera phones to record any instances of police violence whether they are the victim or a bystander.

FBI director James Comey discourages this saying, "scrutiny of police conduct and the threat of exposure through 'viral videos' has generated a chill wind blowing through American law enforcement over the last year."

Even Bogle, a police hater admitted, most of the time there's video, it demonstrates the officer did the right thing.

So maybe the video is the solution. No matter what, though, video evidence will not change the media and put an end to their hate campaign. That is something they have to do on their own. In order for the media to reverse what they have done something they will day admit that they have to do, they need to embrace Rawls's theory. They need to leave race, gender, income level and so on, out of the discussion when it comes to reporting on crimes and law enforcement. In an ideal world, race would not be something that makes our mind think differently about someone or something they did. We would purely judge people on their character. So maybe that is the solution to this problem, and if so, then that is up to the generations and journalists of the future.

Police Forces Face Challenges on All Sides

J. Christian Adams

J. Christian Adams is an attorney who worked in the Department of Justice Civil Rights Division under the administration of President George W. Bush, and the New York Times *bestselling author of* Injustice: Exposing the Racial Agenda of the Obama Justice Department.

The Black Lives Matter movement must guard against becoming an advocacy arm of gangsters and criminals. A recent pistol-whipping of a police officer in Birmingham, Alabama, occurred because police around the country are becoming too afraid to act like police. Portraying criminals as victims and the police as criminals will foster an atmosphere of lawlessness and criminality that will harm every American, particularly those hardest hit by crime.

Janard Cunningham is lucky to be alive. Pulled over by an Alabama police officer for erratic driving, Cunningham exited his vehicle during the traffic stop, aggressively approached the police officer and delivered a debilitating sucker punch to the officer's head.

When any police officer is debilitated by a criminal's blow to his head, it's a life or death moment. Threatening deadly force against an attacker is perfectly reasonable. Even using deadly force to terminate the attack might be justified. But thanks to the fashionable demonization of police officers driven by activists and their enablers in the media, that's not what happened next.

Instead, Cunningham seized the stunned officer's firearm and pistol whipped him senseless. The officer said he didn't defend himself because of fear of what the media and the activists would do to him. "A lot of officers are being too cautious because of what's

"Forget Criminals, Police Now Fear Activists and the Media," by J. Christian Adams, the National Interest, August 22, 2015. Reprinted by Permission.

going on in the media," the unnamed police officer told CNN. "I hesitated because I didn't want to be in the media like I am right now. It's hard times right now for us."

When police officers fear Al Sharpton more than they fear a gangster with a gun, the country has arrived at a dangerous moment.

But Jared Cunningham wasn't alone in his depravity that day. Bystanders joined in. Emboldened by the fashionable hatred of the police, the onlookers didn't render aid to the bleeding officer, instead they snapped photos.

The photos posted on social media show a police officer face down on the concrete. Others show him covered in blood. Priorities, I suppose.

Naturally, the gruesome photos went viral, especially among the anti-police crowd.

"Pistol whipped his ass to sleep," one Facebook user wrote. The photos were passed around Twitter with hashtags such as #FDAPOLICE replacing (or joining) #BlackLivesMatter for a time.

I doubt very much the well-meaning supporters of the Black Lives Matter movement want much attention for their more zealous co-marchers. They've decided to ride this tiger and will find it very difficult to get off, no matter how many police end up hurt or killed.

The Black Lives Matter movement should be careful. In the end, they will lose everything when mainstream America sees more stories of police officers being shot and photos of bloodied detectives. Given a choice between thugs and cops, Americans will ultimately take the side of the police. When it seems the thugs have scored too many scores, Americans will lose all sympathy for those criticizing the police.

But something even more incendiary is in play. The truth is that civil society and domestic tranquility aren't givens. In fact, over the course of history, they are often the exceptions. Violent gangsters acting out is a characteristic of human experience as old as time. It is a dark tendency that systems of law and traditions of order are designed to oppose. When the acts of violent gangsters begin to intermingle with political movements, the risks multiply.

Simply put, the anti-police movement has elements which are both grotesquely violent and other elements which are explicitly political. There doesn't seem to be much effort of the latter to disown the former.

The violent acting in the name of political has always been one of the most dangerous threats to civil society. The danger exists even when the violent purport to act for the cause. Those who advocate for or praise the violence have also fulfilled an essential role historically to aid this menace.

What could be the reason that the movement to "reform" police departments doesn't seem to have the will to jettison every nook and cranny of the violent wing of the movement? I refer to both the overtly violent as well as those who delight in the use of violence against the police. Do the more mainstream and peaceful elements of the Black Lives Matter crowd relish the energy for the cause the nastier allies provide? Or is it merely a delight in payback? After all, on social media, that wicked view of payback is easy to find, as it was in response to the events in Alabama.

You can't find much criticism of this odd, informal and increasingly nasty confederation of police "reformers" among most media. In fact, some media are more likely to criticize anyone who draws attention to the violent side of the anti-police cause than they are likely to dwell on the more uncomfortable trends in the movement.

Doing anything else might expose too much, and trigger a mighty backlash by mainstream America to the growing thuggery on our nation's streets. When that thuggery starts to borrow slogans and memes of an organized, and heretofore, lionized cause, that backlash might not be far off.

CHAPTER 2

Is Excessive Force Ever Justified?

Overview: There Is a Place for Use of Deadly Force

Eric Tucker

Eric Tucker covers the Justice Department for the Associated Press in the Washington, DC, area.

WASHINGTON — The law gives police officers latitude to use deadly force when they feel physically endangered, but there's far less legal flexibility when it comes to opening fire at fleeing individuals. Here's a look at legal issues raised by Saturday's police shooting in South Carolina in which video recorded by a bystander shows a black man being shot in the back and killed as he runs away.

Is there a federal legal standard to judge the appropriateness of police use of force?

Yes. The Supreme Court held in a 1989 case, Graham v. Connor, that the appropriateness of use of force by officers "must be judged from the perspective of a reasonable officer on the scene," rather than evaluated through 20/20 hindsight.

That standard is designed to take into account that police officers are frequently asked to make split-second decisions during fast-evolving confrontations, and should not be subject to overly harsh second guessing. The Justice Department cited that legal threshold last month when it declined to prosecute former Ferguson, Missouri police officer Darren Wilson in the shooting death last summer of an unarmed black 18-year-old.

Can police officers shoot at fleeing individuals?

Only in very narrow circumstances. A seminal 1985 Supreme Court case, Tennessee vs. Garner, held that the police may not shoot at a fleeing person unless the officer reasonably believes that

"When Can Police Use Lethal Force Against a Fleeing Suspect?" by Eric Tucker, NewsHour Productions LLC, April 8, 2015. Reprinted by Permission.

the individual poses a significant physical danger to the officer or others in the community. That means officers are expected to take other, less-deadly action during a foot or car pursuit unless the person being chased is seen as an immediate safety risk.

In other words, a police officer who fires at a fleeing man who a moment earlier murdered a convenience store clerk may have reasonable grounds to argue that the shooting was justified. But if that same robber never fired his own weapon, the officer would likely have a much harder argument.

"You don't shoot fleeing felons. You apprehend them unless there are exigent circumstances—emergencies—that require urgent police action to safeguard the community as a whole," said Greg Gilbertson, a police practices expert and criminal justice professor at Centralia College in Washington state.

Gilbertson said he thought the video of the shooting of Walter Scott in North Charleston, South Carolina, was "insane" given what he said was the apparent lack of justification.

Though the legal standard has been established, courts continue to hear cases involving use of force against fleeing felons under a variety of circumstances. Just last year, the Supreme Court sided with police officers who were sued over a high-speed, two-state chase in Arkansas that ended with the deaths of the fleeing driver and his passenger.

In cases where police officers are not supposed to use deadly force against a fleeing person, what should they do?
Each case involving a suspect who flees the police, whether in a car or on foot, poses a balancing test for an officer, said Chuck Drago, a police practices expert and former Oviedo, Florida, police chief.

"Am I creating more of a danger by chasing this person than if I let this person stay at large?" Drago said. "Especially in a vehicle pursuit, is it worth risking everyone on the road to catch this guy?"

In a pursuit on foot, the more reasonable option might be to call for backup, including perhaps with a police dog, so that other officers can set up a perimeter and trap the suspect, Drago said.

In the South Carolina case, the former lawyer for the North Charleston officer, Michael Slager, said Monday that Slager felt threatened and had fired because Scott was trying to grab his stun gun—an older model that would have had to have been manually reloaded. But if the stun gun was on the ground at the time Scott fled, Drago said, then "there is no longer a threat. The threat is gone."

There's also no indication on the video that after the physical encounter between the men, where the officer has said he believed Scott had tried to get ahold of his stun gun, that he shouts any instructions.

Is there a role for federal involvement in the investigation?
The FBI and the department's Civil Rights Division are working together to examine the case. Though the officer faces a state murder charge in South Carolina, the federal government will be looking at the shooting for potential civil rights violations.

That means federal agents and prosecutors will be looking to establish not only that Slager killed Scott, but that the officer willfully deprived Scott of his civil rights and used more force than the law allowed.

The Justice Department often investigates police use of force, though not all investigations result in prosecution. In some cases, such as in the 1991 beating of Rodney King in Los Angeles, federal prosecutors have moved forward either with their own investigation or prosecution after the conclusion of a state case.

Context Is Key: Police Are Human and Often Forced to Act

Kazu Haga

Kazu Haga is a Kingian Nonviolence trainer based in Oakland, California, who works with youth, incarcerated populations, and activists. He is also the founder and coordinator of East Point Peace Academy.

I t's okay mommy…. It's okay, I'm right here with you…"

Those were the words of four-year-old Dae'Anna, consoling her mother Lavish Reynolds after she witnessed the police shoot and kill her boyfriend Philando Castile.

Those words are now scarred into the psyche of America, much like words that came before it: "Hands up, don't shoot." "I can't breathe." "It's not real."

If you haven't realized that the system of policing isn't working for the black community, you haven't been paying attention. Just hours after the killing of Alton Sterling, a four-year-old child witnessed someone getting shot and bleeding out while she sat in the backseat. The system didn't work for her, her mother or for Philando Castile. The system didn't work for Alton Sterling, or for Mike Brown, or for Freddie Gray or for countless others.

But here's something we miss in this climate of police violence: the system of policing isn't working for those working in law enforcement either. It doesn't serve anyone.

When I watched the video taken by Lavish Reynolds, I was blown away by the cool and calm demeanor in her voice and how it was offset by the complete panic in the voice of the officer. His was filled with fear.

And why wouldn't it be? Behind that trigger lies a man who just took the life of another man in front of a child. I've worked with enough people in prison, as well as veterans who have taken the lives of others, to know that no human being is immune to the fear, guilt and shame that comes with the taking of another's life.

The system of policing is one that relies on violence, fear, repression and a colonizer mentality. But the individuals who are employed to enforce that mentality are human beings with a human psyche, just like any other. It's silly to assume that these men and women aren't impacted by the violence they witness and participate in every day. No human being can participate in the levels of heightened violence that police are engaged in without being affected by it.

The tragedy in Dallas is a response from a people within a community that has lived with that fear and violence for generations. If you belong to a community that is constantly facing murder, incarceration and dehumanization, it should come as no surprise when members of that community decide that they have had enough and react with violence. It is tragic, yet should not be surprising if you can see their perspective. Similarly, just because police experience that violence from "the other side," it should not surprise us that it may affect them in similar ways, and that they may similarly react with outbursts of violence.

Martin Luther King, Jr. wrote that "the white man's personality is greatly distorted by segregation, and his soul is greatly scarred." He said that the work of defeating segregation was for the "bodies of black folks and the souls of white folks." He understood that to be a white supremacist, to hold hatred in your heart for so many and to inflict violence on others destroys your soul.

Others have written about the history of policing in the United States — especially in the South — and its roots in the slave patrol. So it should come as no great leap to consider that participating in policing in 21st century America could scar one's soul.

This is not about being an apologist for the individuals responsible for the killing of black life. It is not about comparing the suffering of black communities to that of law enforcement. But in nonviolence, we know that if you don't understand the perspective of those who you are in conflict with, you do not understand the conflict. You do not need to agree with, excuse or justify the other's perspective, you simply need to understand it so you can see the complete picture.

And part of the picture looks like this: Cops are human. They work for an institution with historical ties to slavery and a long legacy of racism. They are indoctrinated in a culture of "us vs. them," of doing "whatever is necessary so you get home," of fear, distrust, and dehumanization of those deemed as being on "the other side." They are taught to fear for their lives. They are trained almost exclusively in tactics of violence and repression. They are sent into situations of conflict every day with those limited tools, into communities where they are playing out tensions that have been brewing for hundreds of years.

Looking at that picture, no one should be surprised at incidents of police violence, and we should all understand that to some extent, it is rooted in the spiritual and emotional degradation that results from being immersed in such a violent institution.

I've been thinking lately about Eric Casebolt, the officer who responded to a call at a pool party in McKinney, Texas and proceeded to throw a young girl onto the ground and point his gun at other teenagers.

Casebolt should have been fired immediately, and his record should follow him everywhere, preventing him from ever having employment as a cop or even as a security guard.

If we look more into the history of that conflict, the story of Casebolt's own trauma begins to emerge. The pool party was the third call that he attended to that day. His first was a suicide where he witnessed a man blow his head off in front of his family, and had to console the family. Immediately after, he was called to another attempted suicide, where he had to talk a young girl down from jumping off a ledge — also in front of her family. By the time he reached the pool party, he was an emotional wreck.

Again, that's not to excuse his actions as an individual. But understanding that context and perspective also allows us to point our fingers at the larger culprit: a system of policing that didn't care enough about Casebolt's mental health that they couldn't even give him the rest of the day off. A culture of machismo that doesn't give space for cops like Casebolt to grieve or process what he just went through.

When the system comes together to defend cops like Casebolt, their defense of him is a smokescreen. The system doesn't care about any individuals — the individuals are dispensable. It is trying to distract us from the fact that the system itself is corrupt. If the system truly cared about the people who work in the system, it would create fundamental changes to stop the killings of black people, thereby decreasing the chances of retaliatory killings like the ones in Dallas.

But for us, the more we focus our anger on the individual who pulled the trigger, the more we are letting the system off the hook. And the more the system defends the individual, the more we want to see him or her locked up, as if they are the problem. Hook, line and sinker.

Individual accountability requires healing, and a space for the perpetrator of the harm to feel remorse for their actions. I've learned over time that people can't empathize with the pain that they caused until their own pain and story has been honored. So, can we build a movement that honors the pain of the officers, creates spaces to help them see the pain that they cause, and — following the example of former Baltimore officer Michael Wood — allows them to defect from a system that doesn't serve them either?

And can we hold that level of compassion without pacifying our righteous indignation towards a system that doesn't value human life? How do we build a fierce and powerful resistance movement that addresses the individual and the system? What does it look like to hold individuals accountable with compassion, and systems accountable with indignation?

#AltonSterling, #PhilandoCastile and #Dallas are sobering reminders that violent institutions are causing human death on all sides. And until we find justice for all people, their spirits will be with us, nudging us to answer those questions.

Civilians Can Use Deadly Force, Too

Robert Farago

Robert Farago is the founder and publisher of a website called the Truth About Guns (TTAG). His writing experience stems from his time as a news writer for WBRU-FM in Providence, RI.

Your legal right to use deadly force (i.e. shoot someone) varies from state to state. This article gives you some basic guidelines on the legal use of deadly force. What you are about to read is not legal advice. I am not a lawyer. After you finish here, Google "deadly force YOUR STATE HERE" and read your state's law. If you have any questions or concerns, contact your local NRA chapter. Take a Use of Deadly Force class. Do not call the police. Just as they have no legal obligation to protect you (true story) they have no legal obligation to give you accurate legal advice. OK, so, we begin with another disclaimer . . .

At the end of the proverbial day, if you shoot someone, a number of people will decide whether or not you were legally justified in doing so. The police will decide whether or not to arrest you. A District Attorney/Prosecutor will decide whether or not to charge you with a crime. Should the incident proceed to trial, a judge or jury will decide whether or not you had a legal right to fire your weapon.

In most states, juries use the "reasonable person" standard to determine guilt or innocence. Would a reasonable person in the same circumstances fire their weapon? We're talking the totality of circumstances here. Considerations include your age, weight, height, sex, physical health and life experience; the bad guy(s) age, height, sex, appearance and actions; the type of threat (weapons?); the reason for the threat (robbery? rape? knockout game?). The

"A Closer Look at a Big Question: When Can You Legally Shoot Someone in Self-Defense?" by Robert Farago, Thetruthaboutguns.com, March 13, 2015. Reprinted by Permission.

exact situation as it unfolded: who, what, when, where and why. Everything. All of it.

Regardless of the reasonable person standard, you should know your state's rules for the legal use of deadly force. You should have these rules clear in your mind before you pick up your gun. If you know when you can bring our weapon to bear on the bad guy or guys, you will do so with less doubt and more confidence. If you know when you can't shoot, you'll keep your powder dry and avoid a whole lot of legal, moral and financial trouble down the line. Maybe . . .

Generally speaking, lethal force is permissible when you or other innocent life face an imminent, credible risk of death or grievous bodily harm, and imminence is imminent. Let's start at the end of that sentence and work our way to the beginning.

"Imminence is imminent"

People use the word "imminent" to describe something they think is about to happen. "I could tell the bad guy was about to attack me from the way he looked at me and his racial slurs." So "the attack was imminent." Nope. The word "imminent" means something quite specific when it comes to armed self-defense. It means an attack in the process of happening. Hence the codicil "and imminence is imminent." You weren't thinking someone was about to attack you. They were in the act of attacking.

Even if it's a group of previously convicted criminals revving their Harleys and shouting that they're going to gut you like a fish, even if it's a blood-soaked knife-wielding maniac waving a knife in the air, you can't shoot them until they begin their attack.

OK, you can. As I said above, it's up to the police, prosecutor, judge or jury to decide if your use of lethal force was justified. They may or may not make allowances for your state of mind. Even so, the mental tripwire for the using your firearm should be "I'm being attacked." You may have the legal right to "stand your ground," but up to that point, escape and evade are your two best friends.

"Death or grievous bodily harm"

If someone attacks you with a pillow, you are not at risk of death or grievous bodily harm. Unless you're lying in a bed and they're using the pillow to try to smother you. If someone pinches you, you are not at risk of death or grievous bodily harm. Unless they're "pinching" your testicles with a pair of pliers. If someone slaps you, you are not at risk of death or grievous bodily harm. Unless they're slapping you with brass knuckles.

See how that works? The possibility of suffocation, broken bones, head injuries, stab wounds, gunshot wounds – they all count as grievous bodily harm. Bumps and bruises don't. It's simple common sense, really. Unless it isn't . . .

You, reasonable person that you are, may have had good reason to think you were in danger of death or grievous bodily harm when you fired your weapon, but actually weren't. Very much. If at all. Or were you? How bad was that fight when you pulled your gun – or how bad was it going to get? (See: use of force continuum.)

What if someone enters your house to rob it but they don't actually attack you? Is that cause enough to shoot them? What if they're carrying a gun? What if you warn them to leave and they don't? What if you don't warn them and lay in wait and then shoot them? It's a legal grey area or, if you prefer, a minefield.

That said, in most but not all jurisdictions, your home is your castle; invaders are viewed as an inherent lethal threat (hence "the castle doctrine"). When you use your firearm outside the home, things can get awful hinky, legally speaking. For example, some states apply the castle doctrine to your car or place of business. Some don't.

Either way, this raises an important point: just because you can shoot someone legally doesn't mean you should. Unless the threat of death or grievous bodily harm is completely clear, you may want to escape, evade or, perhaps, brandish your weapon as a warning.

[Note: some states allow the use of lethal force for other reasons, such as preventing kidnapping, theft or arson. Check your state's laws.]

"Credible threat"

If a 10-year-old boy points a pen knife at you from twenty feet away, that's not a credible threat of death or grievous bodily harm (nor is imminence imminent). If a bad guy steps out of the shadows right in front of you with a kitchen knife aimed at your heart, that is. If someone points a gun at you intending to do you harm (as opposed to, say, sweeping you with their muzzle at a gun range), that's a credible threat. It all comes down to how likely the threat is to be successful if you don't stop it by deploying lethal force.

Again, your opinion on the matter is subject to the authorities' and jury's opinion under the "reasonable person" standard. Again, they will base their decision on the totality of the circumstances surrounding the defensive gun use. And again, that determination varies according to state law and the local culture. Remember: there are states where you have a so-called "duty to retreat." These states are likely to have a high standard for what constitutes a credible threat. And imminence. And grievous bodily harm.

"Innocent life"

If you're minding your own business, you are the innocent party. You are legally allowed to use lethal force to stop an imminent, credible threat of death or grievous bodily harm—provided imminence is imminent, subject to the usual caveats and official second-guessing. Same goes if someone else is minding their own business when they face an imminent, credible threat of death or grievous bodily harm, and imminence is imminent. You are legally allowed to use lethal force to stop the threat against them—subject to the usual caveats and official second-guessing.

While you have an excellent idea of when you're innocent (e.g., not starting a fight), using your gun to protect "other innocent life" is fraught with danger. Let's say you see a woman being attacked by two men. The violence is severe and she's screaming rape. You shoot the attackers to save the victim's life. Only the "attackers" were undercover police trying to arrest a perp. Good luck with that. By the same token, let's say you shoot a Stop 'N Rob clerk thinking he was a robber (they'd switched places during the robbery). That's not going to go well for you, either.

The best bet is to refrain from using lethal force unless you've seen the whole incident from its inception. In fact, I'd like to end this article with a simple warning: shooting a bad guy or guys can create enormous disruption to your life; morally, spiritually, financially, socially and legally. It may not, but it can.

If you face an imminent, credible threat of death or grievous bodily harm and imminence is imminent, chocks away— remembering that some state laws on lethal force impose a duty to retreat. If, however, you can find a way not to use lethal force and avoid injury to yourself or other innocent life, that's your best option. In any case, know the law on lethal force in your state and do your best to avoid stupid people in stupid places doing stupid things. That is all.

Excessive Force Knows No Bounds

Martin Kaste

Martin Kaste is a correspondent on NPR's national desk, covering law enforcement and privacy as well as news from the Pacific Northwest. He's been with National Public Radio since 2000.

The Justice Department has released a scathing report that accuses the Chicago Police Department of systematic use of excessive force.

SCOTT SIMON, HOST:
The U.S. Justice Department has released a scathing report that accuses the Chicago police of systematic use of excessive force. The report is the Obama administration's final significant action in its campaign for police reform. NPR's law enforcement correspondent Martin Kaste joins us now. Martin, thanks so much for being with us.

MARTIN KASTE, BYLINE: You're welcome.

SIMON: Let's remember the background. What exactly has the Justice Department said about Chicago police?

KASTE: Well, this report comes after that really controversial shooting of the young black man named Laquan McDonald. He was shot back in 2014. When the video finally came out, it looked as though he was fleeing police at the moment he was shot. And the outrage caused by that video triggered the Justice Department to do this investigation. And after about a year of investigating, the DOJ is now saying that excessive force happens too much, that the Chicago Police Department uses deadly force and other kinds

"Chicago Police Often Used Excessive Force, DOJ Report Finds," by Martin Kaste, NPR, January 14, 2017. Reprinted by Permission.

of force, such as the use of Tasers, too frequently in cases often where it's not justified. And they say the police department doesn't do an adequate job investigating those uses of force, disciplining officers or training them.

SIMON: What concrete effect could a report like this have on the everyday function of the police department?

KASTE: Well, that's where the whole question of the timing of this report really becomes important because normally, at least over the last eight years or so, a report like this would have been the first step in the Justice Department's pressure on a local police department to reform. The report would be sort of a public shaming, which would then set things up for the city to enter into negotiations to set up what's called a consent decree. And what a consent decree is is basically a legally binding plan for reform with a federal judge monitoring the process. They don't have one of those yet in Chicago. They basically ran out of time. And it's not clear right now whether the new administration when President Trump takes office will be interested in having one. The nominee to run the Justice Department, Jeff Sessions, has expressed some skepticism over the past about consent decrees. He says sometimes they could, in his words, smear a whole police department because of the misdeeds of a few officers.

SIMON: Chicago's Mayor Emanuel has made a point of starting reforms in training and police oversight. Do they really need a consent decree with the federal government?

KASTE: Well, reformers say that historically those noble intentions in many big cities that have had these problems - those noble intentions kind of fade away over time, that the pressure against reform is pretty intense. This is how the U.S. attorney in Chicago, Zach Fardon, put it yesterday.

(SOUNDBITE OF ARCHIVED RECORDING)

ZACH FARDON: The problems that we discovered are long-standing, in some cases decades old, and prior efforts at reform in Chicago's history, there have been many. They have not gotten the job done.

KASTE: So reformers would say without that extra pressure from a federally enforced consent decree reforms don't happen. I should point out that the mayor, Mayor Rahm Emanuel, has said he wants to enter into a binding consent decree, but he says he can't negotiate the Trump administration side of that. If they're not interested, it may not happen.

SIMON: Yeah. What's been the reaction from the Chicago Police Department, especially when we take a look at the enormous increase in shootings and murders over the last year and the accusation against the police that they haven't been patrolling as vigorously as they used to?

KASTE: Well, Chicago cops have really low morale right now, and that's something even this report talks about. And when you talk to regular cops, many of them say they think that surge in violence is in part because of all the criticism they've been undergoing for the last few years, that they've been told to basically hold off on some basic kinds of street enforcement because they're worried about the backlash. And they say that that's emboldened those young people who carry guns to go ahead and shoot each other. That's not a narrative that the current Justice Department buys into, but there's a chance that the next administration would see their point.

SIMON: NPR's Martin Kaste, thanks so much.

KASTE: You're welcome.

Law Enforcement Needs Fundamental Changes

Irving Joyner

Irving Joyner has been a professor at the North Carolina Central University School of Law since 1982, and from 1984–1992, he served as the associate dean.

In recent months, the nation has witnessed several killings of African-American individuals by White police officers and a White security guard. These include the recent killings of Oscar Grant in California, Trayvon Martin in Florida, Eric Garner in New York, Michael Brown in Missouri, and Tamir Rice in Ohio. In each case, the established criminal justice process failed to evidence a serious intent to prosecute the offending officers, sparking vocal nationwide protests. Had civilians committed the same acts as these officers, they would have been prosecuted for a criminal offense.

In most cases, the protests that arose after these deaths were immediate, in large part because many African Americans and people of color have seen close family members or friends become the victims of police misconduct. Indeed, misconduct is an issue of epic proportions in minority communities. In the vast majority of these cases, law enforcement and prosecutorial officials have failed or simply refused to pursue criminal charges against the offending police officers. In those few cases where prosecutors have brought criminal charges, district attorneys have not vigorously pursued the cases and they have generally not produced guilty verdicts.

This failure of justice is not a recent issue. I vividly recall the shooting death of my 17-year-old cousin in LaGrange, N.C., when I was seven years old. My cousin Bobby Joyner was murdered by a White police officer on a Wednesday night as he walked home from choir rehearsal. He was shot in the driveway of the all-White high school, where he bled to death. After he died, his body was dragged across the street and placed under the bedroom window of a White woman's home; the window screen was slit with a knife in an attempt to make it appear that Bobby was breaking into her home. An African-American garbage collector was awakened from his home and directed to cover the puddle of blood in the school driveway with dirt. As soon as the sun rose the next morning, family members took pictures of the murder scene, which clearly showed the covered-up blood puddle and visible tracks where the body had been dragged through the dirt and grass and placed under the window of the house.

In 1952, there were no federal laws to protect African Americans or enable prosecutions against White police officers. In those days, during Jim Crow, you could not expect White police departments to arrest or charge any White person for crimes against African Americans. Nor could you expect a White prosecutor to prosecute a White person for committing a crime against an African American. The law, then and now, grants prosecutors complete authority to determine who will be prosecuted, and no one can interfere with that power. It is also important to remember that in 1952, there were very few African-American police officers, and perhaps no African-American prosecutors, anywhere in this country.

Therefore, despite the best efforts of my grandfather and other town leaders, their organized campaign to obtain an investigation was ignored. Instead, they immediately became the target of police intimidation and harassment. Their experience illustrated the stubborn reality, almost 100 years after Dred Scott v. Sanderford, that African Americans had no legal rights that White governmental officials were required to respect or acknowledge.

In 2015, a time when there are civil rights laws on the books and many police departments and prosecutors' offices are racially integrated, you would not expect the responses to police killings of African Americans to meet the same fate as in 1952. But the failure to investigate is the same today as it was then—except now it is a national problem.

The simple explanation for this problem is that this nation's laws are deliberately designed to protect police officers from prosecution for misconduct. This protection has served to embolden police officers in contact or confrontations with African Americans and other minorities.

An examination of North Carolina law shows why there are very few prosecutions. North Carolina's laws are no isolated phenomenon—the vast majority of states rely on a similar scheme. With respect to the officer authorization to use force, most State laws simply say that police officers are privileged to use force against civilians. Under the North Carolina statute, a police officer is justified in using physical force upon a person when, and to the extent that, the officer reasonably believes it necessary to prevent the escape or make the arrest of a person who the officer reasonably believes has committed a criminal offense. In addition, the officer is justified in using force to defend himself or a third person from what he reasonably believes to be the use or imminent use of physical force while making an arrest.

The basic notion is that the officer is authorized to use force when in the officer's judgment, he reasonably believes that the force used is necessary to effect an arrest or to discharge an authorized duty. This subjective standard differs from an objective standard where the officer's conduct is measured against what a reasonable, well-trained police officer, acting appropriately, would have done under similar circumstances. Pursuant to this subjective standard, when the officer believes that he or a third person is in danger of harm, he can, under the law, use any amount of force which that officer believes is necessary to overcome the danger or harm threatened. In determining the amount of force to be used, the officer may consider all of the surrounding circumstances, including the nature of the perceived offense, the person's reputation, the words or actions used by the person and whether he is armed or suspected of being armed.

Where a police officer uses fatal force, the controlling statutory standard is similar. A police officer is justified in using deadly or fatal force when it appears to the officer to be reasonably necessary to defend himself or a third person from what the officer reasonably believes to be the use or imminent use of deadly physical force. In addition, the officer can use fatal force to effect an arrest or prevent the escape of a person who the officer reasonably believes is attempting to escape by the use of a deadly weapon, or to prevent the escape of a person from custody imposed upon him as a result of a felony conviction. In the landmark case of *Tennessee v. Garner*, the United States Supreme Court declared it unconstitutional for a police officer to use fatal force for the sole purpose of apprehending a person suspected of committing a crime. However, that Court did affirm an officer's use of fatal force if it was necessary to prevent an escape where the suspect posed a significant threat of death or serious bodily injury to the officer or to a third person.

These statutory authorizations place the officer on an elevated scale of protection from prosecution that civilians do not enjoy. Officers are trained to understand how much authority they have, and they understand that courts are going to extend the benefit of the doubt to them unless an officer has abused his authority. The authorization for an officer to use reasonable force to complete an arrest is not intended to serve as a justification for willful, malicious, or criminally negligent conduct; nor does it authorize the officer's use of "excessive" force. Yet, in practice, it has been used to justify police killings. The mere fact that a person has committed a crime—or appears to the officer to have committed a crime— does not authorize a police officer to kill him. Even when the person resists arrest, this does not automatically justify an officer's use of fatal force, since resisting does not always involve physical threats and assaultive conduct. Clearly, the fact that the person is an African American or another racial minority member does not justify an officer's decision to kill that individual. The critical test is whether the person is engaged in actual conduct, at that moment, which places the officer or a third person in imminent danger of serious bodily injury or death. This determination is based upon the "totality of the circumstances," which always focuses on exactly what the person is doing to endanger the personal safety of the officer or a third party.

Many people are under the mistaken impression that a person must willingly and immediately submit to police authority whenever the police officer makes contact with them. As a matter of law, unless a police officer has obtained a reasonable suspicion to detain a person or probable cause to arrest a person, no lawful authority can be asserted over any individual. In the absence of reasonable suspicion or probable cause to believe that the person is engaged in criminal conduct, a police officer has no legal authority to interfere with a person's movements.

This lawful expectation leaves room for any person to dissent or resist police conduct directed toward them. Although it is not the case in most states, in North Carolina, a person has the authority to resist an unlawful arrest. However, even in North Carolina, an individual never knows when an illegal arrest is occurring and acts at their peril in choosing to resist an arrest. Individuals are expected to raise all legal challenges to an arrest or an officer's use of force in court. However, this assumes the individual is alive to make it to court and is represented by an attorney who can gather witnesses to provide factual information that supports the challenge.

The laws regarding the use of force do not favor civilians over police officers. Police officers abuse their legal authorization to the use of force, which aligns with an aggressive, militarist policing culture and style that is deliberately designed to deter individual resistance. These aggressive practices demonstrate forceful conduct in order to convince civilians that they should not resist the police. Often times, officers will even engage in "swarm" tactics where they use as many officers and weapons as possible to convince people that they are overpowered or can be overpowered. Consequently, individuals are pushed out of positions where they can observe what is occurring or are prevented from recording the events. Using this strategy, police officers are able to isolate individuals who have been targeted for a police operation from others who might serve as eyewitnesses or who could lodge an on-the-spot protest of inappropriate conduct.

Where a police officer uses any degree of force, fatal or non-fatal, against an individual, it is not necessary that the person was actually armed, dangerous or presently engaged in the commission of a crime in order to justify the officer's conduct. The United States Supreme Court has determined that a reasonable belief by the officer that force was necessary, even if based on a mistake of fact or of the applicable law, is sufficient to satisfy the constitution. Based on the North Carolina statute, as long as the officer himself reasonably believed that the person posed a threat or danger of serious bodily injury or death, he would be justified in using fatal force.

Moreover, prosecutors, who work closely with individual officers, are not inclined to prosecute police officers for their aggressive use of power. Moreover, a prosecutor's decision not to prosecute cannot be reviewed or reversed by anyone. At the next election, voters can vote in a new prosecutor, but there is no legal authority that can compel a prosecutor to pursue criminal charges against a police officer. On the other hand, if the prosecutor decides to prosecute an officer, a grand jury must also affirm that decision. To further compound this lack of oversight, there is no independent or meaningful complaint process or redress apparatus within local police departments. In fact, the filing of a misconduct complaint with the Internal Review Unit usually will intensify the complaining party's persecution and harassment.

Finally, the courts have created a "qualified immunity" status for police officers. With "qualified immunity," the law protects an officer against civil rights claims, except in those very rare cases where the particular conduct committed by the officer violates clearly established law. If those particular facts or law have not been previously found to be illegal through some judicial adjudication, the officer is protected from a civil rights lawsuit even being filed. Under "qualified immunity," most legal challenges never go to trial and escape an adjudication based upon the legal merits. By the same token, prosecutors enjoy "absolute immunity" from a civil rights claim for the refusal to investigate a police misconduct claim or to prosecute the offending police officer. Even where a legal claim against a police officer survives the "qualified immunity" barrier and is allowed to go to trial, it can take years and huge amounts of money before a final verdict is rendered.

In order to deal with police misconduct, it is necessary to make fundamental changes to the laws, authority, and procedures which presently protect police officers and enable them to use indiscriminate physical force against individuals. Anything short of a comprehensive change of the laws regularly used to justify the unjustified killings of African Americans and other racial minorities will achieve no more than spitting in the wind. As such, efforts to alter and bring about fundamental change of the police culture and its use of force will continue to frustrate people.

As a beginning proposition, fundamental changes should include:

A change in the legal standard that authorizes the use of force—from the police officer's subjective judgment to that of an objective, reasonably well-trained officer;

1. The creation of an independent civilian review board that has the ability to review all police misconduct, has subpoena power, is staffed by trained professionals and can administer discipline for police misconduct and improper training;

2. The provision of authority for the state attorney general to appoint a special prosecutor to investigate and prosecute wrongful death claims;

3. Requirements that police officers reside in the cities or towns where they are employed;

4. Requirements of written permission for police officers to search a person's residence or automobile where a search warrant has not been previously issued;

5. Requirements of the use of car and body cameras while

officers interact with individuals, and of discipline for those officers who fail to use these devices;

6. Requirements of psychological examinations for all officers, bi-annual re-evaluations, and the administration of mental assessments after an officer has been involved in a fatal force incident;

7. Requirements that all officers and administrators to successfully participate in ongoing racial sensitivity and conflict resolution training every five years, more often if needed;

8. An insistence that police departments become more racially and culturally diverse across each administrative level;

9. A re-examination of the question of who controls the police, and placement of the police under the authority of a citizen commission.

The reforms listed above represent a mere starting point and should not be viewed as exhaustive. It is important to understand that modern-day police authority and the use of force have no constitutional origin or justifications. Rather, they has been created by statutes and endure only by public consensus. As presently used, the powers of the police have grown to the extent that they dwarf the constitutional rights and protections which citizens enjoy. As such, the legal limits of this authority should be re-examined.

Police Officers Have Incentives to Engage in Misconduct

Jonathan Blanks

Jonathan Blanks is a research associate in the Cato Institute's Project on Criminal Justice and also serves as the managing editor of PoliceMisconduct.net. His research focuses on law enforcement practices, overcriminalization, and civil liberties.

During any given criminal case, certain facts in police testimony that appear to be banal or happenstance—such as the placement of a hand or someone dropping a bag of drugs—seem reasonable when taken by themselves.

But looking at police testimony in similar cases, if some facts continue to appear in case after case, an observer may come to a disquieting conclusion: police are lying.

"Testilying" is the colloquial term for the police practice of lying on official documentation or in court under oath (i.e., perjury). Typically, testilying is used to justify searches in drug cases that would otherwise be deemed illegal.

The exclusionary rule, established in *Mapp v. Ohio* (1961), states that evidence gathered from a search that violates the Fourth Amendment cannot be used in court against a defendant. If, however, a police officer testifies that he saw the drugs dropped into plain view, he has probable cause—and thus, legal permission—to conduct a search without a warrant.

Some criminal justice observers think it may be the most common manifestation of police misconduct.

Alex Kozinski, now-chief judge of the U.S. Court of Appeals for the Ninth Circuit once said, "It is an open secret long shared by prosecutors, defense lawyers and judges that perjury is widespread among law enforcement officers." Many commentators in the legal

"Reasonable Suspicion: Are Police Lying in Use of Force Cases?" by Jonathan Blanks, Cato Institute, January 7, 2015. Reprinted by Permission.

community agree, though there is no consensus about what to do about it.

The repeat players in the criminal justice system naturally recognize testimony they hear over and over again. Unless drug dealers magically became klutzier after Mapp, there is strong reason to believe so-called dropsy testimony has become a widespread and illegal institutional work-around to the Fourth Amendment.

Perjury—lying in court under oath—is a crime in any circumstance, whether in a misdemeanor drug trial or a capital murder case. Police officers are very rarely charged with perjury in any type of case, despite testilying's ostensible pervasiveness. If testilying is as common as some believe, and police feel immune to perjury prosecutions, the incentive to lie to defend themselves or a colleague in a use-of-force case must be very strong.

Testilying in drug cases strongly suggests police are acutely aware of the evidentiary rules and procedural demands placed on them by legislators and the judiciary. As I noted in my last piece, officers operate with wide discretion within the boundaries of those demands.

In use-of-force cases particularly, giving broad leeway to police officers makes a lot of sense. Unlike members of the public who are free—if not demanded, in some cases—to flee dangerous situations, police officers are tasked to run toward danger for the sake of the citizenry. Police are forced to make split-second judgments on dangers to themselves and others when dealing with a potentially dangerous suspect.

Officers are human and therefore make honest mistakes, and thus the justice system should provide them with a modicum of protection when they make errors that reasonable people would make given the same circumstances.

But just as any power may lead to abuse, so may legal privileges, even those granted with the best of intentions.

The two most prominent Supreme Court cases in use-of-force authority are *Tennessee v. Garner* (1985) and *Graham v. Connor*

(1989). These two cases indeed provide ample protections for police officers with regard to the use of force.

Edward Garner was a teenager fatally shot by Memphis police while fleeing officers after commission of a burglary. In *Tennessee v. Garner*, the Supreme Court held that lethal force may not be used to stop a suspect simply to prevent him from fleeing. The Court writes:"Where the suspect poses no immediate threat to the officer and no threat to others, the harm resulting from failing to apprehend him does not justify the use of deadly force to do so….A police officer may not seize an unarmed, nondangerous [sic] suspect by shooting him dead….[I]f the suspect threatens the officer with a weapon or there is probable cause to believe that he has committed a crime involving the infliction or threatened infliction of serious physical harm, deadly force may be used if necessary to prevent escape, and if, where feasible, some warning has been given." Tennessee v. Garner, 471 U.S. 1 (1985), 9-12.

Notably, the Garner decision exposed the government to litigation for the officer's unreasonable use of force. The Court noted that Garner, being an unarmed young teen of slight physical build who was fleeing police, could have posed no imminent threat to police or others and therefore the use of lethal force was clearly unreasonable.

In Graham, the Court goes further to describe what is and is not a Fourth Amendment violation as a result of excessive force. Perhaps as a surprise to some readers, there is no right against excessive force as such, but rather courts must make after-the-fact determinations of whether seizures (i.e., violence used by police to arrest or detain a suspect) before trial are unreasonable and thus violate the Fourth Amendment. Therefore, even though the officers involved in Graham handcuffed and roughly threw an innocent man suffering insulin shock into a squad car saying, "Ain't nothing wrong with the motherfucker but drunk. Lock the son of a bitch up," the Court ruled his perfectly legal but suspicious behavior—running into and out of a convenience store—led the police officers to reasonably believe that a crime may have been committed and his detainment, however aggressive, was therefore legal.

Simplifying, then, these cases taken together lay out the standards for what is expected of police officers in use-of-force encounters and how their actions should be judged after the fact. Garner outlines the specific conditions that may obviate the prohibition on the use of lethal force against a suspect: the suspect must pose an immediate threat to the officer or the public; be armed and/or dangerous; must threaten the officer with a weapon; or had committed a crime causing serious physical harm. Additionally, when possible, the officer should warn the suspect before opening fire. Graham dictates that any actions taken by a police officer must be "objectively reasonable" given the circumstances presented to pass Fourth Amendment scrutiny.

Just as we see the fit-the-requirement nature of dropsy testimony to avoid Mapp's exclusionary rule, we may expect to see similar accounts of officer-involved shootings in regard to Garner and Graham.

Put another way, the requirements of these cases may inadvertently provide a template for officer testilying in use-of-force cases.

Sure enough, these shootings tend to include many of the following details: a description of the officer's imminent fear for his own safety; phrases such as "the suspect made furtive movements" or "charged the officer"; the suspect exhibited a superhuman resistance to nonlethal force such as physical restraint, TASER, bean-bag rounds, or even bullets; the suspect ignored repeated and explicit demands to put hands up; or the suspect "raised his weapon." In addition, some version of the phrase "he reached for his waistband," "he reached under the seat," or "he was reaching for my gun" will demonstrate the officer had reason to believe the suspect was reaching for a firearm, satisfying Garner's imminent safety requirement, even though the suspect may turn out to be unarmed.

These statements paint a picture of an officer waiting until the last possible moment and exhausting all other available means before deploying lethal force. Indeed, this is what we want our officers to do when faced with mortal danger. A recollection of facts in this way—absent proof to the contrary—is often enough to clear a police officer, given the cultural inclination to give police the benefit of the doubt and the case law currently governing use-of-force incidents.

Surely, sometimes those facts recited in these investigations are entirely true. But given the relative uniformity of testimony in case after case, it is unreasonable to believe each officer is following the guidelines time after time.

The quick-to-violence escalations we see on video of officer-involved shootings and other uses of force unambiguously confirm this. Add the continued patterns of abuse in minority communities, the resentment that treatment engenders, and the disproportionate rate at which people of color are shot by police, the numerous protests around the country demonstrate a concentrated and growing skepticism the police narratives in use-of-force incidents.

One may wonder how exactly these stories acquire such relative uniformity across jurisdictions, and whether testilying has, in fact, bled into use-of-force cases.

In his grand jury testimony, then-Ferguson police officer Darren Wilson recounted that he methodically and rationally went through the checklist of possible non-lethal defenses against his alleged attacker Michael Brown as he was in imminent fear for his own life. Perhaps that's true.

But Wilson also testified:"Yeah, just from what I have been told about the incident originally, is that you are supposed to have 72 hours before you are actually officially interviewed, recorded statement and all of that. You tend to remember more through a couple sleep cycles then what you do as soon as it happens. It is a traumatic event, a lot of details kind of come as one detail."

Police officers may receive such "cooling off" periods before giving statements in criminal or internal investigations of which they played a role. Although not codified in Missouri law, this period is just one aspect of a broader program of police protection known as "law enforcement officers' bills of rights." These bills of rights are only statutory in a handful of states, but various protections in them are operative in many jurisdictions as standard operating procedure.

Among the other benefits afforded to police officers is the right to union representation at all questioning by police authorities. This means that during this cooling off period, the officer may discuss the matter with union representatives and, presumably, they will work together to provide the best possible story for the investigators. Such a story would necessarily align with the requirements of Graham and Garner.

Whether Wilson was given this time after initial questioning as a matter of collective bargaining agreement or professional courtesy, it's fair to say most civilian shooting suspects wouldn't hear a detective say, "Go home, sleep on it for a couple days—oh, here's the number of a good defense lawyer—and come back when you get your head right."

Given all this, that Wilson's testimony about the events that led to Michael Brown's death read like a checklist of the most menacing and dangerous behavior imaginable by Brown and, alternatively, that Wilson himself calmly considered and then exhausted every possible non-lethal option before opening fire cannot be surprising.

Again, it could all be true, but the people of Ferguson have plenty of reasons to doubt it.

Positive framing of events so requires no malice, it is natural that someone and his counsel would paint his actions in the best possible light. But it is important to remember that our criminal justice system is based on an adversarial system—prosecution and defense before a neutral arbiter—and prosecutors who regularly depend on police officers as their allies in court are naturally less likely to challenge the credibility of those officers when one of them is accused of wrongdoing.

Moreover, as Garner shows, a finding against the officer further exposes the department and government to costly lawsuits, thereby increasing potential political pressure to exonerate the officer.

In short, police officers are afforded extra protections in use-of-force incidents and, additionally, are less likely to face anyone within the criminal justice apparatus who will strongly challenge their version of events. This creates an environment that implicitly tolerates inappropriate uses of force because of the diminishing likelihood of negative repercussions for those actions.

Police have a dangerous job. Undoubtedly, officers face deadly situations and can be wholly justified in their use of lethal force. And it would be going too far to say that police lawyers, unions, and prosecutors knowingly suborn police perjury.

However, the incentives in jurisdictions all over the country encourage officers to lie, not only in their day-to-day work, but also when their actions result in violence against the public.

The criminal justice apparatus has yet to seriously address police lying in most cases, let alone when police themselves are subjects of criminal investigations. Thus, police officers are incentivized to lie and their institutions are incentivized to protect their officers in use-of-force incidents.

This results in more injustice, less trust in the police, and more dead civilians.

CHAPTER 3

Is Excessive Force a Bigger Problem Now?

Overview: Things Have Changed Since the Early '90s

Nicole Flatow

Nicole Flatow is the editor of CityLab at the Atlantic. *She has also served as the associate director of communications for the American Constitution Society and the deputy editor of ThinkProgress Justice.*

Amadou Diallo. Rodney King. Timothy Thomas. Looking at where we are today in the weeks after the shooting of Michael Brown in Ferguson, Missouri, it can feel like nothing has changed in the way we police the police.

Many things haven't. Juries acquitted police. Cops got their jobs back. And brutality happened again.

Some things have gotten worse. Like police militarization.

But some things have gotten better, or are still moving toward reform in the wake of a prominent brutality incident. A history of these incidents reveals that some major recent police reforms got their start after highly publicized episodes of police violence. But it was only after years or decades and dogged, persistent community-building that some progress started to manifest.

Rodney King, 1991, Los Angeles

Videotape by a bystander captured five officers pummeling Rodney King with batons more than 50 times as he struggled on the ground outside his car. The recording immediately sparked outrage, but anger magnified when the officers who beat King were acquitted by a jury the following year. The acquittal triggered three days of violent riots during which at least 53 people died—and created immense momentum for reform. The cops in that case were ultimately held accountable, when federal prosecutors took up the case and secured convictions of four officers. And by

"What Has Changed About Police Brutality in America, from Rodney King to Michael Brown," by Nicole Flatow, ThinkProgress, September 11, 2014. Reprinted by Permission.

some measures, the LAPD was transformed in the two decades that followed.

Los Angeles was the original militarizer of police, even before the federal government started handing out left-over or used weapons, and before the height of the War on Drugs.

"The LAPD was the godfather of that kind of militaristic response," said John Jay College of Criminal Justice's Joe Domanick, author of a forthcoming book on LAPD reforms and the West Coast Bureau Chief for the Crime Report.

Los Angeles was forced to scale back in some ways after the riots, partially as a result of the Christopher Commission, created in response to the King beating to develop recommendations for reform. But initially, few of the Commission's recommendations were adopted by the city. "The Christopher Commission recommendations laid a foundation but weren't successful in bringing about reform," Domanick said.

One of the most significant reforms that did come out of the Commission was ending the policy of lifetime terms for police chiefs. The police chief who presided during that period and had overseen an era of increased militarization at the Los Angeles Police Department, Daryl Gates, was forced to resign. And thereafter, lifetime terms were over.

In the intervening years, the city took advantage of its prerogative to hire chiefs for five-year terms and then bring in someone new, in a series of chiefs who instituted some change but failed to alter the culture. Domanick said that changed when Bill Bratton became chief more than ten years later in 2002 and instituted what is known as community policing. Underlying this approach is the idea that police can rarely solve public safety problems alone, and require the input of various stakeholders to come up with solutions that might be resolved by social services or other measures instead of a heavy police hand. Bratton was hired as a reformer chief, after a series of incidents of corruption emerged known as the Rampart scandal. "He started to make a dent in the culture of occupying force," said Domanick, whose forthcoming book is titled, *Blue: The Ruin and Redemption of the LAPD.*

When Bratton arrived, the stage was set for real change because of a few other intervening developments. Five years after King's death, the city finally instituted a recommendation to create an independent inspector general to review the Department. In 1994, Congress passed provisions in the Crime Control Act meant to address police misconduct in a more systematic way, partially on the momentum of the Diallo beating. One provision gave the Department of Justice the power to bring civil suits against local police departments that exhibited a "pattern and practice" of excessive force or other constitutional violations, and the Department used that power to enter into a settlement known as a consent decree with Los Angeles.

This provision is perhaps among the most far-reaching remedies for holding entire police management structures accountable. Typically, Justice Department investigations that find constitutional violations result in agreements known as "consent decrees" that avert litigation by agreeing to federal monitoring and reforms. Common reforms include changes to police training, stronger mechanisms for complaints against officers, and improved supervision. A Vera Institute study of the first consent decree in Pittsburgh, Pennsylvania, found that use of force incidents declined after the consent decree ended, and that the city largely succeeded in meeting DOJ goals, but that citizens still perceived police as sometimes using excessive force, particularly against minorities.

It was in executing his city's consent decree that Bratton transformed the LAPD. "It is like night and day," Jeff Schlanger, who was hired to monitor the LAPD in 2001, told NBC News. As in Ferguson, what was most lost after the Los Angeles riots is what is known as "police legitimacy"—community trust in the police that underlies all of their work. Bratton instituted an era of communication and respectful interaction between individuals and police, creating a department that reflected the community and building relationships with community leaders. He even demonstrated some inclination for holding officers accountable. After a violent police response to 2007 immigration rallies in McArthur Park, Bratton announced immediate investigations and several officers were eventually demoted or fired.

But many things remained unresolved. For one thing, the mechanisms for policing the police didn't improved much. A Human Rights Watch report noted that "at risk" LAPD officers who frequently use significant force continued to act with impunity, and officers were not frequently punished for misbehavior, either internally or by the courts. For another, some tactics embraced by Bratton have created their own set of hostilities with minority communities, as a result of policies that see targeting low-level offenses in high-crime areas as key to thwarting larger crime, Domanick said.

When this policy is not implemented with constant rigor, these police stops can also lead to unnecessary police violence and even death, as in the case of Ezell Ford, shot while reportedly laying on the ground after a routine police stop for still-undisclosed reasons.

Amadou Diallo, 1999, New York City

Plainclothes officers from the New York Police Department shot street vendor Amadou Diallo just outside his Bronx apartment building after they mistook his wallet for a gun. These officers, too, were acquitted at trial.

Then-police Commissioner Howard Safir instituted some changes after weeks of protest, including adding more minority officers to the special "Street Crimes" unit whose officer had shot Diallo and requiring all officers in the unit to wear uniforms.

But Darius Charney with the Center for Constitutional Rights said these fixes were nothing more than cosmetic, and lamented that the city initiated nothing like the Christopher Commission to reform itself. Weeks later, his organization honed in on what was perceived as the real issue uncovered by the shooting—the aggressive over-use of police stops. CCR filed a lawsuit to force reform, triggering a campaign against stop-and-frisk overuse in the NYPD that is still continuing.

At the time of the police shooting, the overwhelming police presence in some minority-heavy communities was a revelation to the general public. CCR's lawsuit sought data on the numbers and types of stops. For years, production of this data was delayed even after the City Council passed a data collection law. But in 2006, outrage once again bubbled up when Sean Bell was killed by undercover cops in the wee morning hours of his wedding day, and the New York Civil Liberties Union compelled the city to release the data.

What this data revealed was that "stop-and-frisk was actually getting worse, not better," Charney said. The number of police stops had increased more than five-fold over the course of just five years, and they were just as racially skewed as they had ever been. With facts finally in hand, CCR filed a second lawsuit that resulted in a long-awaited victory when a federal judge held last year that the New York Police Department had engaged in unconstitutional racial profiling.

Even now, the court has not yet enforced that order as the police unions hold up final resolution by attempting to intervene on the appeal that Mayor Bill de Blasio has already dropped. But using the momentum of that litigation, advocates were also able to successfully campaign for new city legislation to hold police accountable. One new bill creates an inspector general to oversee NYPD. Another allows citizens to sue the police department for profiling not just based on race but also sexual orientation, religion, housing status, and other discriminatory categories.

"We have been able to I think working in tandem with advocates and organizers outside of the courtroom really make meaningful change," Charney said of the city's progress.

But progress hasn't solved many things yet. In the weeks before Brown's death, police killed Eric Garner using an illegal chokehold, after they stopped him for suspected sale of untaxed cigarettes. That death was ruled a homicide by the medical examiner.

Police accountability is still wanting in New York, with a citizen review board whose recommendations for officer discipline are often ignored by the police commissioner, and no neutral mechanism for prosecuting police. "We for many years have really pushed for a state-level agency … to prosecute crimes for municipal level police officers," Charney said, citing the inherent bias prosecutors have in favor of the police.

And as a Twitter campaign gone wrong in April demonstrated, NYPD still hasn't quite come to terms with its tainted reputation.

Timothy Thomas, 2001, Cincinnati

The big-city police departments in Los Angeles and New York have been under close watch both before and after these incidents, as they face the unique challenges and advantages of concentrated metropolitan areas. But perhaps an incident that most closely mirrors that in Ferguson is the 2001 shooting of Timothy Thomas by police that triggered riots in Cincinnati, Ohio. Thomas, a 19-year-old with an infant son, started to run when an officer approached him on the street outside a nightclub. The officer called in back-up, a chase was on, and shots were fired with almost no information about Thomas. Cops said they thought Thomas was reaching for a gun but none was ever found.

The officer in that case, too, was acquitted. But even before the verdict, community members responded to the shooting with intense riots and an economic boycott, exposing a history of racial tensions with police. Thomas was the 15th black man who died during a police confrontation in the six years before the riot. And by the time of Thomas' death, the perception was that Cincinnati faced intractable tensions between citizens and police that couldn't be fixed by yet another investigation or report. But public outrage along with federal intervention created the momentum for a different, expansive settlement in 2002 from litigation that started even before Thomas was killed. The pressure became so great that police stopped resisting, and started collaborating.

As a result of agreements involving several advocacy groups

and the Department of Justice, officers were trained on how to choose less-lethal force, and how to deal with the mentally ill and those under the influence of drugs or alcohol. They even created a mental health response team. They were not just given Tasers, but also exhaustive training on when they could use them and how. If they used a Taser, they had to document their use. And if their record didn't match what was being reported, an investigation would ensue. Cars were equipped with dash cameras. They took "community policing seriously," doing walk-throughs of neighborhoods with residents, holding community meetings, and responding to community problems with nuanced solutions. Cincinnatti's police chief has so embraced the reforms in the Collaborative Agreement that he takes a copy everywhere he goes.

And one more thing. Police were actually held accountable. Mike Brickner, senior policy director of the ACLU of Ohio, said one of the persistent problems the city encountered was that a few bad actors were committing egregious acts again and again without punishment, and giving the entire department a bad name as a consequence. But after Thomas' death, a Citizen Police Review Board was formed that seemed to actually have buy-in from the police department. Officers were disciplined, given new training, or fired. Police and particularly police unions had resisted the accountability mechanisms "tooth and nail" for years before Thomas' death. But when public pressure became overwhelming, Brickner says even police unions fell in line. And in the end, many officers ended up liking the review mechanism, finding that it could be just as useful to exonerate an officer who had been wrongfully accused as to punish an officer for wrongdoing.

"I never thought I'd hear myself say this, but those riots were some of the best things that ever happened: They taught us who we are and what mattered," Kathy Y. Wilson, who for years wrote a local column called "Your Negro Tour Guide," told the *Washington Post*.

"The outcomes of the Cincinnati collaborative agreement were pretty astounding and we were really pleased with them," Brickner said. But he cautions against any reform plan that pretends there is an easy fix. "I will not pretend that this is an easy process," Brickner said. His advice to other cities: If it goes too smoothly, you're probably not really instituting change. "It takes a lot of time and a lot of hard work and there will certainly be for anyone going through a process like this moments where it's very difficult and very painful," he said.

Last month, two Cincinnati officers shot Donyale Rowe to death after he was pulled over for failure to signal. Immediately after the incident, the police chief named the officers involved and published their performance reviews. He said Rowe had a gun, and he released video of the incident from the dash cam. No tension erupted.

"Even where there is a strong intervention and things have changed significantly, I think it's unrealistic to say that there is never going to be another police problem or another issue that crops up," he said. "But I think what has changed is that there are much fewer of them." And when incidents do come up, "police also have the tools and the training and the mutual understanding of how to talk about these issues … so that they can be quickly navigated through and done in a way that communities can agree on and live with and that they don't boil over in the way they dd in 2001."

And police accountability remains one of the most sticky problems. A 2008 *Cincinnati Enquirer* review found that while 35 police officers were fired over a 20-year period, 19 of the 25 who appealed the decision to an arbitrator got their jobs back, with heavy backing from the police union. Many of the others who didn't win faced criminal charges that made it "difficult … or impossible" for them to get their job back.

Post-Ferguson

The city of Ferguson will have its own local reforms to consider, as the council has already passed several bills to establish a police review board, and set limits on excessive court fines and fees exposed after Brown's death. If past experience is any indication, reforming the police department is possible over the course many years and many battles.

But nationally, problems persist. "This is a very systemic problem in just about every community throughout the United States," Brickner said.

And even in communities that have seen dramatic change, there are as many holes left to be filled as there have been reforms. One is the intransigent, incredible challenge of holding police accountable. Police unions exercise strong influence over many local boards that decide whether cops get to keep their jobs. Juries tend to side with police. And the law overwhelming favors the police. UC Irvine law school dean Erwin Chemerensky, who has long followed this issue, wrote after Brown's death that "the officer who shot Michael Brown and the City of Ferguson will most likely never be held accountable in court" due to doctrines from the Supreme Court down that weigh against holding officers accountable.

Another is a culture that embraces guns. Police are given a lot of leeway to use deadly force, in many instances when the public perception is that other lesser measures might do. As CNN's Mark O'Mara noted after Brown's death, "Cops are doing the job we told them to do."

Riots in Ferguson have also exposed to America the extreme militarization of police forces that has only grown since the past waves of police shootings. And the racism in the criminal justice system persists, both overtly, and implicitly, even as more whites than ever believe the criminal justice system is no longer biased.

But there are reasons to be hopeful. For one thing, criminal justice reform is increasingly becoming a bipartisan issue. Even Rep. Paul Ryan (R-WI) became one of a growing number of congressional Republicans who have called for criminal justice reform. Domanick said he was also encouraged that there was outrage at Ferguson's police militarization across the political spectrum. For another, reform options exist that didn't before, such as body cameras for police. In fact, it is the emergence of mobile recording devices that has exposed some of the recent violent incidents—and debunked any attempts by police to skew the facts.

In the case of Ferguson, U.S. Attorney General Eric Holder has announced he will initiate an investigation of the city's "patterns and practices" in addition to the separate criminal investigation of the Brown case. In fact, Holder has taken on a new tone for the country's top law enforcer that acknowledges the United States epidemic of discriminatory and overly punitive criminal punishment.

But underlying all of this is the segregation and oppression that was unveiled in Ferguson. A Washington Post investigation last week revealed that these underlying problems still persist in Cincinnati, meaning that while police were indeed reformed, fixing the racial tensions that existed in 2001 Cincinnati is "a job unfinished." Even Cincinnati's black police chief says he fears his own son's encounters with the police.

"The cultural disconnect is very real; you have the weight of generations of abuse on African Americans," Cincinnati Police Chief Jeffrey Blackwell told the *Washington Post* after Brown's death.

"[T]he mentality is that these lives in the ghetto are not to be valued," added Domanick. "Policing and violence are only symptoms of this larger problem. We're gonna have problems. But at least we're starting to know now what works in terms of reducing crime short term and long term and what works in terms of community policing and good community relations."

Some Data Proves Excessive Force Has Increased

Celisa Calacal

Writer Celisa Calacal serves as the opinion editor of Ithaca College's award-winning student newspaper the Ithacan *and also writes for ThinkProgress and Alternet.*

This is how many people police have killed so far in 2016

The year isn't over yet, and police have already killed at least 1,023 people—many of whom were unarmed, mentally ill, and people of color.

This number comes from the *Guardian*'s police killings database, but the Killed by Police database counts 1,096 people who have died at the hands of police so far this year. The *Washington Post* reports that 908 people have been shot and killed by cops.

Going by the *Guardian*'s count, Native Americans and Black people are being killed at the highest rates in the United States. 215 Black Americans have been killed by police so far this year, at a rate of 5.38 deaths per million. February and March were the deadliest months this year, with 100 people killed by police in each month. Police have killed 32 people in December so far.

[...]

The slight discrepancies in numbers between Killed by Police and the *Guardian* reflect differences in how each outlet collects data about police killings. Killed by Police is mainly open-sourced and also relies on corporate news reports for its data on people killed by police. For its database, the *Guardian* relies on traditional reporting on police reports and witness statements, while also culling data from verified crowdsourced information using regional news outlets, research groups, and reporting projects that include Killed by Police.

"This Is How Many People Police Have Killed so Far in 2016," by Celisa Calacal, ThinkProgress, July 5, 2016. Reprinted by Permission.

There has always been a high volume of police killings, although damning videos, photos, and news reports highlight officer violence—especially against people of color—now more than ever. But what's become an even more alarming trend is the number of officers involved in these killings who receive minor to no punishment.

According to the *Wall Street Journal*, 2015 saw the highest number of police officers being charged for deadly, on-duty shootings in a decade: 12 as of September 2015. Still, in a year when approximately 1,200 people were killed by police, zero officers were convicted of murder or manslaughter, painting the picture that officers involved in killing another person will not be held accountable for their actions.

In 2016, several officers have gone to trial but none of them received jail time. Here are some of the most egregious examples of cops who haven't been penalized for killing:

William Porter, Edward Nero, and Caesar Goodwin—Baltimore, Maryland

Freddie Gray was apprehended by police during a bike patrol on April 12, 2015, when a violent arrest left him unable to walk on his own. On the way to booking, no officer put a seat belt on Gray, causing him to be thrown around the van with no help received from any of the officers. In total, there were six officers involved in his death, and three have been tried so far. But during those three trials, which spanned from December 2015 to June, none of the officers were convicted.

The trial of Officer William Porter ended in a hung jury in December, amounting to no action being taken against Porter unless a second trial scheduled for later this year finds him guilty. In May, Officer Edward Nero was declared not guilty of all criminal charges against him—second-degree assault, reckless endangerment, and misconduct in office. Nero was one of the first officers to encounter Gray during his arrest and helped load Gray into the police van, where he was not secured with a seat belt.

On June 23, the latest trial in Gray's case found Officer Caesar Goodwin not guilty of second-degree depraved heart murder, reckless endangerment, second-degree assault, and manslaughter. Goodwin drove the police van where Gray suffered the spine injury that ultimately led to his death, didn't secure the 25-year-old's seat belt, and waited to call a medic when Gray was in distress. Goodson faced the most serious charges of the six officers.

Peter Liang—New York City

In April, two months after a jury convicted him of manslaughter and official misconduct, former NYPD Oficer Officer Peter Liang was sentenced to five years probation and 800 hours of community service.

Liang is responsible for fatally shooting 28-year-old Brooklyn resident Akai Gurley last November, in the dark stairwell of a public housing building. While Liang was in the building, the rookie cop claimed he accidentally fired his gun and the bullet ricocheted off the wall before striking Gurley in the heart. Gurley was innocent of any wrongdoing and unarmed when he was killed.

During the trial, Liang claimed the shooting was accidental, but was convicted of manslaughter in February. The former officer was also convicted of official misconduct for failing to provide any sort of medical assistance to Gurley as he lay bleeding on the staircase. Following his conviction, Liang was fired from the NYPD.

Just before his sentence was handed down, the manslaughter charge was reduced to criminally negligent homicide. And despite being convicted of manslaughter, Brooklyn District Attorney Ken Thompson announced in March that jail time for Liang should be taken off the table. He recommended six months of house arrest, five years of probation, and 500 hours of community service, instead.

Liang was the first NYPD officer convicted of an on-duty shooting in the past decade.

Mark Ringgenberg and Dustin Schwarze—Minneapolis, Minnesota

In March, Hennepin County Attorney Mike Freeman announced that the two officers involved in the fatal shooting of 24-year-old Jamar Clark will not be facing any criminal charges for their actions. Clark, who was unarmed, died from a gunshot to the head when Schwarz fired his gun 61 seconds after arriving on the scene.

According to the county attorney, Clark was resisting arrest and attempted to grab Ringgenberg's gun. Despite this claim, several witnesses say that Clark was already handcuffed. Although placed on administrative leave following the shooting, both officers returned to desk duty in January.

Two weeks prior to the decision, Freeman announced that Hennepin County, including Minneapolis, will no longer use grand juries to determine whether cops involved in fatal shootings should be indicted. "I concluded that the accountability and transparency limitations of a grand jury are too high a hurdle to overcome," he said. Beginning with Clark's case, Freeman's office would decide to indict in the future.

The policy shift was made in response to pressure from Black Lives Matter activists who protested against grand jury proceedings in the Clark case.

The Poor Suffer the Most at the Hands of Police

Gabriel Black

Gabriel Black works for International Youth and Students for Social Equality, the youth and student organization of the Socialist Equality Party. He also writes for the World Socialist website.

At least 1,152 people were killed by police in the United States in 2016 according to the tracking site killedbypolice.net. While the total number of killings documented is slightly down from 2015's total of 1,208, police continued to kill at the rate of three people every day.

The number of people killed by police every year in the United States far dwarfs those killed by police in every other major advanced capitalist country. In 2015, for example, US cops killed 100 times more people than German police, despite the United States having only about four times Germany's population. Meanwhile in the United Kingdom only 14 people were killed by police in 2014.

Paul Hirschfield, a sociologist at Rutgers University, found that the US police shot and killed at a ratio of 3.42 people per million inhabitants per year. In contrast, Denmark had a ratio of 0.187; France, 0.17; Sweden, 0.133; Portugal, 0.125; Germany, 0.09; Norway, 0.06; Netherlands, 0.06; Finland, 0.034; and England and Wales, 0.016.

The overwhelming and often deadly violence meted out by American police is, among other things, an expression of the brutal and tense state of class relations in the United States. Large sections of the working class live in or near poverty with basic needs like clean water, nutritious food, a job, health care, a good place to live and an education beyond reach.

"US Police Killed More Than 1,150 in 2016," by Gabriel Black, World Socialist website, January 4, 2017. Reprinted by Permission.

The state, in turn, has responded with brute force, cutting access to basic social services and spending billions of dollars upgrading and militarizing the nation's police force. This has included the mobilization of the National Guard and the imposition of states of emergencies to quell protests against police violence in recent years.

The United States is a country where fraud, bribery, deception and outright theft, all on a massive scale, are standard business practices for the major banks and corporations. Meanwhile the working class is held to an entirely different standard, in which execution without trial by a police officer is an increasingly common punishment for the smallest of misdemeanors.

The end of the year is an opportunity to assess this mass loss of life and clarify the political issues at stake in this state sanctioned murder.

According to the *Washington Post*, which runs its own database on the number of people shot and killed by police (not just killed), 24 percent of the victims of police shootings and killings were black in 2016. That is 232 people out of 957 total shot and killed. In 2016 African Americans were shot at a rate double their percentage share of the total population.

While the media discussion around police killings and the protests by the Black Lives Matter organization has focused on the disproportionate rate at which blacks are killed by police, the largest share, 48 percent, are white.

As the World Socialist Web Site has emphasized, "Blacks are killed by police at a much higher rate than their proportion in the population, an indication that racism plays a significant role, but the number of white victims demonstrates that class, not race, is the more fundamental issue."

The exclusive focus on race by the pseudo left and the Democratic Party establishment conceals the most fundamental issue, that of class.

While the *Post* does not track the class of those killed going through each killing, though, case-by-case, one would be hard pressed to find people from the upper classes, let alone better off sections of workers and professionals, regardless of the color of their skin. Those who are killed are often from the lowest sections of the working class, and often its most vulnerable layers: the unemployed, the mentally ill, those living in the poorest neighborhoods, both rural and urban, and the homeless.

For example, of the 957 killed, 240 had clear discernible signs of mental illness—that is, 25 percent of the victims.

Of the victims, 441 were not armed with a gun, 46 percent of those killed. One-hundred seventy people were armed with a knife. And, 44 had a toy weapon of some kind. Forty-seven were neither armed nor driving a car in a way the police deemed dangerous.

Sixty-five were driving cars, causing the police to categorize the vehicle as a weapon. However, in many instances there is no evidence to show that a vehicle acted as a weapon. For example, Christian Redwine, a 17-year-old white male, was shot after a car-chase in which Redwine crashed. He was unarmed and was suspected of stealing the vehicle.

Another notable fact is that 329 of the victims were fleeing, about 34 percent of the victims.

These cumulative statistics show the willingness of police to quickly kill people who pose little to no threat to them.

Police killings should be considered in the broader context of punishment for the most vulnerable and impoverished. In the United States, over 2 million people are in federal or state prisons. Furthermore, 4.75 million are on probation or parole. This means that about 7 million people, 3 percent of the adult population, have been or are in prison.

As in the case of police killings, many of these people have been locked up for shoplifting, grand theft auto and robbery. Many others are incarcerated for drug possession and use.

While millions of destitute and hopeless people in the United States are brutally punished for relatively minor infractions, the real criminals, those in the Bush and Obama administrations responsible for wars of aggression that have cost the lives of hundreds of thousands in the Middle East, as well as the bankers who crashed the economy in 2008, have reaped the benefits of their much more serious crimes.

No amount of police training, community engagement or racial bias classes will end police killings. The deaths are born out of much more fundamental political and economic realities than what this or that police officer feels and thinks. In 2017, amidst a worsening political and economic crisis, the state will be even more ready to kill, harass and imprison the poorest section of the population.

Being Unarmed Makes No Difference

Adam Hudson

Adam Hudson is a journalist whose work has appeared in multiple media outlets, including AlterNet, Truthout, teleSUR English, the Nation.

Police officers, security guards, or self-appointed vigilantes extrajudicially killed at least 313 African Americans in 2012 according to a recent study. This means a black person was killed by a security officer every 28 hours. The report notes that it's possible that the real number could be much higher.

The report, entitled "Operation Ghetto Storm", was performed by the Malcolm X Grassroots Movement, an antiracist grassroots activist organization. The organization has chapters in Atlanta, Detroit, Fort Worth-Dallas, Jackson, New Orleans, New York City, Oakland, and Washington, D.C. It has a history of organizing campaigns against police brutality and state repression in black and brown communities. Their study's sources included police and media reports along with other publicly available information. Last year, the organization published a similar study showing that a black person is killed by security forces every 36 hours. However, this study did not tell the whole story, as it only looked at shootings from January to June 2012. Their latest study is an update of this.

These killings come on top of other forms of oppression black people face. Mass incarceration of nonwhites is one of them. While African Americans constitute 13.1% of the nation's population, they make up nearly 40% of the prison population. Even though African Americans use or sell drugs about the same rate as whites, they are 2.8 to 5.5 times more likely to be arrested for drugs than whites. Black offenders also receive longer sentences compared to whites. Most offenders are in prison for nonviolent drug offenses.

"1 Black Man Is Killed Every 28 Hours by Police or Vigilantes: America Is Perpetually at War with Its Own People," by Adam Hudson, AlterNet, May 28, 2013. Reprinted by Permission.

"Operation Ghetto Storm" explains why such killings occur so often. Current practices of institutional racism have roots in the enslavement of black Africans, whose labor was exploited to build the American capitalist economy, and the genocide of Native Americans. The report points out that in order to maintain the systems of racism, colonialism, and capitalist exploitation, the United States maintains a network of "repressive enforcement structures". These structures include the police, FBI, Homeland Security, CIA, Secret Service, prisons, and private security companies, along with mass surveillance and mass incarceration.

The Malcolm X Grassroots Movement is not the only group challenging police violence against African Americans. The Stop Mass Incarceration Network has been challenging the policy of stop-and-frisk in New York City, in which police officers randomly stop and search individuals for weapons or contraband. African-American and Latino men are disproportionately stopped and harassed by police officers. Most of those stopped (close to 90%) are innocent, according to the New York Civil Liberties Union. Stop Mass Incarceration also organizes against the War on Drugs and inhumane treatment of prisoners.

Along with the rate of extrajudicial killings, the Malcolm X Grassroots Movement report contains other important findings. Of the 313 killed, 124 (40%) were between 22 and 31 years old, 57 (18%) were between 18 and 21 years old, 54 (17%) were between 32 and 41 years old, 32 (10%) were 42 to 51 years old, 25 (8%) were children younger than 18 years old, 18 (6%) were older than 52, and 3 (1%) were of unknown ages.

A significant portion of those killed, 68 people or 22%, suffered from mental health issues and/or were self-medicated. The study says that "[m]any of them might be alive today if community members trained and committed to humane crisis intervention and mental health treatment had been called, rather than the police."

Forty-three percent of the shootings occurred after an incident of racial profiling. This means police saw a person who looked or behaved "suspiciously" largely because of their skin color and attempted to detain the suspect before killing them. Other times, the shootings occurred during a criminal investigation (24%), after 9-1-1 calls from "emotionally disturbed loved ones" (19%) or because of domestic violence (7%), or innocent people were killed for no reason (7%).

Most of the people killed were not armed. According to the report, 136 people or 44%, had no weapon at all the time they were killed by police officers. Another 27% were deaths in which police claimed the suspect had a gun but there was no corroboration to prove this. In addition, 6 people (2%) were alleged to have possessed knives or similar tools. Those who did, in fact, possess guns or knives were 20% (62 people) and 7% (23 people) of the study, respectively.

The report digs into how police justify their shootings. Most police officers, security guards, or vigilantes who extrajudicially killed black people, about 47% (146 of 313), claimed they "felt threatened", "feared for their life", or "were forced to shoot to protect themselves or others". George Zimmerman, the armed self-appointed neighborhood watchman who killed Trayvon Martin last year, claimed exactly this to justify shooting Martin. Other justifications include suspects fleeing (14%), allegedly driving cars toward officers, allegedly reaching for waistbands or lunging, or allegedly pointing a gun at an officer. Only 13% or 42 people fired a weapon "before or during the officer's arrival".

Police recruitment, training, policies, and overall racism within society conditions police (and many other people) to assume black people are violent to begin with. This leads to police overacting in situations involving African-American suspects. It also explains why so many police claimed the black suspect "looked suspicious" or "thought they had a gun". Johannes Mehserle, the white BART police officer who shot and killed 22-year-old Oscar Grant in January 2009, claimed Grant had a gun, even though Grant was subdued to the ground by other officers.

Of the 313 killings, the report found that 275 of them or 88% were cases of excessive force. Only 8% were not considered excessive as they involved cases were suspects shot at, wounded, or killed a police and/or others. Additionally, 4% were situations were the facts surrounding the killing were "unclear or sparsely reported". The vast majority of the time, police officers, security guards, or armed vigilantes who extrajudicially kill black people escape accountability.

Over the past 70 years, the "repressive enforcement structures" described in the report have been used to "wage a grand strategy of 'domestic' pacification" to maintain the system through endless "containment campaigns" amounting to "perpetual war". According to the report, this perpetual war has been called multiple names — the "Cold War", COINTELPRO, the "War on Drugs, the "War on Gangs", the "War on Crime", and now the "War on Terrorism". This pacification strategy is designed to subjugate oppressed populations and stifle political resistance. In other words, they are wars against domestic marginalized groups. "Extrajudicial killings", says the report, "are clearly an indispensable tool in the United States government's pacification pursuits." It attributes the preponderance of these killings to institutionalized racism and policies within police departments.

Paramilitary police units, known as SWAT (Special Weapons and Tactics) teams, developed in order to quell black riots in major cities, such as Los Angeles and Detroit, during the 1960s and '70s. SWAT teams had major shootouts with militant black and left-wing groups, such as the Black Panther Party and Symbionese Liberation Army (SLA) in 1969 and 1974, respectively. SWAT teams were only used for high-risk situations, until the War on Drugs began in the 1980s. Now they're used in raids—a common military tactic—of suspected drug or non-drug offenders' homes.

The War on Drugs, first declared by President Richard Nixon in 1971, was largely a product of US covert operations. Anticommunist counter-revolutionaries, known as the "Contras", were trained, funded, and largely created by the CIA to overthrow the leftist Sandinista government of Nicaragua during the 1980s.

However, the CIA's funding was not enough. Desperate for money, the Contras needed other funding sources to fight their war against the Sandinistas. The additional dollars came from the drug trade. The late investigative journalist Gary Webb, in 1996, wrote a lengthy series of articles for the San Jose Mercury News, entitled "Dark Alliance", detailing how the Contras smuggled cocaine from South America to California's inner cities and used the profits to fund their fight against the Sandinista government. The CIA knew about this but turned a blind eye. The report received a lot of controversy, criticism, and tarnishing of Webb's journalistic career, which would lead him to commit suicide in 2004. However, subsequent reports from Congressional hearings and other journalists corroborated Webb's findings.

Moreover, major banks, such as Wachovia (now part of Wells Fargo) and HSBC have laundered money for drug dealers. Therefore, the very threat that the Drug War claims to eliminate is perpetuated more by the National Security State and Wall Street than by low-level street dealers. But rather than go after the bigger fish, the United States has used the pretext of the "war on drugs" to implement draconian police tactics on marginalized groups, particularly poor black communities.

In 1981, President Ronald Reagan passed the Military Cooperation with Civilian Law Enforcement Agencies Act, which provided civilian police agencies equipment, training, and advising from the military, along with access to military research and facilities. This weakened the line between the military and civilian law enforcement established by the Posse Comitatus Act of 1878, a Reconstruction-era law forbidding military personnel from enforcing domestic laws. Five years later, in 1986, Reagan issued National Security Decision Directive 221, which declared drug trafficking a national security threat to the United States. This militarized the U.S. approach to drugs and overall policing. Additionally, the global war on terror and growth of the National Security State expanded this militarization of domestic police under the guise of "fighting terrorism".

The adoption of military tactics, equipment, training, and weapons leads to law enforcement adopting a war-like mentality. They come to view themselves as soldiers fighting against a foreign enemy rather police protecting a community. Nick Pastore, a former Police Chief of New Haven, Connecticut from 1990 to 1997, turned down military equipment that was offered to him. "I turned it all down, because it feeds a mind-set that you're not a police officer serving a community, you're a soldier at war," he told the New York Times. He said "tough-guy cops" in his department pushed for "bigger and more hardware" and "used to say, 'It's a war out there.'" Pastore added, "If you think everyone who uses drugs is the enemy, then you're more likely to declare war on the people." Mix this war-like mentality with already existing societal anti-black racism and the result is deadly. Black people, who, by default, are assumed to be criminals because of their skin color, become the victims of routine police violence.

The fact that a black person is killed by a police officer, security guard, or vigilante every 28 hours (or less) is no random act of nature. It is the inevitable result of institutional racism and militaristic tactics and thinking within America's domestic security apparatus.

A Decline in Interaction Leads to a Decline in Deadly Force

Steven Malanga

Steven Malanga is a published author, the George M. Yeager Fellow at the Manhattan Institute, and senior editor at the City Journal. *He writes about the intersection of urban economies, business communities, and public policy*

When Congress passed the Violent Crime Control and Law Enforcement Act in 1994, legislators mandated that the attorney general begin studying and reporting on excessive use of force by police. Soon after, the Bureau of Justice Statistics developed a series of recurring studies that measured everything from police behavior in specific situations, like traffic stops, to incidents in which police use force. Much of the data was based not on reports by local police departments, but on direct surveys of citizens, providing some 20 years of information on how the police interact with American citizens, and how those citizens see the police.

If Congress believed that this new data might provide some context and insight for national debates about the use of force by police, such as the one we're having now in the wake of grand jury decisions not to indict police officers for their role in deadly incidents in Ferguson and Staten Island, legislators were largely mistaken. After the Ferguson grand jury made its ruling, President Obama told the nation that "the law too often feels like it's being applied in a discriminatory fashion." Since the Ferguson incident involving Michael Brown and officer Darren Wilson last August, the New York Times has published stories about communities where minorities get stopped more frequently than whites, implying racial discrimination. But these stories ignore Bureau of Justice Statistics data showing that crime victims disproportionately

"What the Numbers Say on Police Use of Force," by Steven Malanga, Manhattan Institute for Policy Research, Inc, December 4, 2014. Reprinted by Permission.

identify minorities as perpetrators of crime, too. Senator Rand Paul has even used Ferguson to launch an attack on the war on drugs, saying that it puts the police in a difficult situation in dealing with the public—though drugs had little to do with the confrontation between Brown and Wilson (except as they may have influenced Brown's aggressive behavior).

Despite such pronouncements, two decades of data on police interactions with the public don't support the idea that something extraordinary is afoot, that the police are becoming "militarized" as President Obama has suggested, or that distrust between police and local communities has produced an enormous spike in conflicts. By contrast, the data show that significant crime declines have been accompanied by a leveling off and then a reduction in confrontations with the police, as reported by Americans of all races.

After the 1994 legislation passed, Justice Department researchers began exploring ways to study the issues as Congress had mandated. In 1996, they produced a preliminary report on police/citizen interactions that broadly estimated that some 45 million Americans had some type of contact with law enforcement during the preceding year. Of those 45 million, the study found, slightly more than half a million reported that the police had used force against them. This initial study, regarded as experimental, wasn't detailed enough to say much more and was subject to large margins of error, but it led to a series of more comprehensive and in-depth reports, produced from 1999 through 2011.

What's striking in the progression of these later studies is a steady decrease in the number of people having interactions with the police—from about 45 million in 2002 to 40 million in 2011—or from about 21 percent of the 16-and-older population to about 17 percent. One clear reason for the decline has been the corresponding drop in crime: the number of people reporting crimes or other problems to the police fell by about 3.6 million from a peak in 2002. More important, perhaps, was that reports of use of force by police also fell, from 664,000 in 2002 to 574,000 in a 2010 report. Those declines occurred across all races. The number of African Americans reporting that police used force against them fell from 173,000 to 130,000. Among whites, the number has dropped from a peak of 374,000 to 347,000.

Since 1999, Justice Department studies have also measured how police and citizens interact during more mundane encounters, like traffic stops—vastly expanding the data about how citizens who otherwise don't have cause to deal with the police might see their performance. In the most recent survey, in 2011, 88.2 percent of those stopped by the police said they thought officers acted properly. There were few significant distinctions by race. Nearly 83 percent of African Americans judged police behavior to be proper, for instance. The study also asked citizens whether they thought the police had stopped them for a "legitimate" reason—and here the data on race is particularly interesting. Some 80 percent of all drivers viewed their stops as legitimate, compared with 68 percent of African Americans. But the study also asked drivers to report the race of the officers who stopped them, and African Americans were just as likely to say that stops initiated by white officers were legitimate as those initiated by black officers. Similarly, white drivers saw no difference in how they were treated by white officers or black officers on this question.

Since 1994, Washington has produced other legislation meant to monitor how local law enforcement behaves. In 2000, for instance, Congress passed the Death in Custody Act, which mandated that the Justice Department collect data on deaths in local and state prisons, including data by race. These data show no startling trends that might raise flags about how those arrested and incarcerated locally get treated. Average mortality in local prisons measured per 100,000 prisoners has decreased from 151 in 2000 to 128 in 2012. Among African Americans, average mortality has dropped from 127 per 100,000 to 109.

These data are particularly instructive in the context of another series of Justice Department surveys, which ask Americans whether they have been victimized by crime. Those who say yes are then asked to identify the race of their attacker. In a 2008 survey, 58 percent of violent crime victims of identified the perpetrators as white, and 23 percent as black. That compares with a national population 74 percent white and 12 percent black. (After 2008, questions about the race of offenders disappear from the victimization data on the FBI's website.) Police frequently point to this survey and others like it to explain that stop rates and arrest rates are higher for minorities because crime rates are higher in minority areas. Victims disproportionately identify perpetrators as minority.

Still, surveys like the victimization report haven't stopped some activists from advocating a form of law enforcement that expects police stops and arrests to mirror the population at large, rather than to reflect a police response to reports of crime. In the aftermath of Ferguson, Attorney General Eric Holder said that he intended to wipe out racial profiling. But as a 1999 Justice Department study on traffic enforcement made clear, racial differences alone in stops or arrests by police "may not signal racial profiling." The study went on to clarify that "to form evidence of racial profiling," the data would also have to show that "Blacks and/or Hispanics were no more likely than whites to violate traffic laws," but were still targeted more frequently than whites. That distinction, which puts stops and arrests within the context of violations committed by a group, has been lost in much of today's media discussion on policing.

National statistics and trends, of course, don't obviate the need to investigate individual acts of force by the police, especially when they result in the death of a citizen. Clearly, even more precise, improved statistics are needed. We don't have good national data on how often police officers discharge their weapons, for example, so we don't know how that changes over time. And as the Wall Street Journal has noted, the FBI's statistics on justifiable homicides by the police nationwide are inaccurate, thanks to a lack of standards in how police departments categorize and report those incidents.

Some of the data reported by large police departments suggest that it's possible to make strides in these areas. New York City keeps detailed records about the use of guns by police officers on duty. Since 1991, the peak of crime in New York, the number of yearly shooting incidents by NYPD officers has declined by more than two-thirds, from 332 to 105. The number of individuals shot and killed by police officers has fallen from 39 to 16. Something similar might be afoot nationally, but we don't have the data to know.

Even if we did, none of this information will make much difference if politicians, activists, and the media keep ignoring it because it doesn't fit the prevailing narrative.

Portland Can Serve as an Example to Other Police Forces

Maxine Bernstein

Writer Maxine Bernstein has been covering crime, police, and law enforcement for the Oregonian *since 1998.*

A Portland Police Bureau analysis shows the bureau's use of force has dropped 35 percent since 2008, according to a four-page report released Wednesday.

The data shows there were 675 use of force incidents by Portland police in 2011, down from 1,039 in 2008.

It's not clear from the report what the bureau's use of force incidents include, but the report specifically notes that the data excludes an officer's pointing of a firearm.

It also presents a graphic that shows that 3.9 percent of arrests in 2011 involved force, down from more than 4 percent of arrests in each of the three prior years.

Portland Police Chief Mike Reese credited policy, training and supervision changes for the drop in use of force.

They include new training for sergeants on when to walk away from certain suicide calls if the person is not a risk to themselves or others; dispatchers' training to divert certain mental health crisis calls from police to the county's crisis line and their mental health workers; and increased internal police bureau reviews of officer use of force.

The report says the bureau is planning to create a "mental health crisis triage desk," but doesn't explain what services it will provide.

Bureau spokesman Sgt. Pete Simpson said the bureau's crisis intervention coordinator is trying to work out some agreement that would allow information on a caller's mental health history to be shared immediately at a new "mental health crisis triage desk." This triage desk would assist in getting a person help, rather than sending a police car out.

"Since 2008, there has been a concerted and growing effort to emphasize de-escalation tools and a confrontation management approach in community contacts to minimize the need for the use of force," the report says.

The brief report was released Wednesday as a federal investigation continues in the bureau's use of force, and as some officers and rank-and-file union leaders are questioning what the chief's standard is regarding police use of deadly force.

Reese testified last fall during fired Officer Ronald Frashour's arbitration hearing that Aaron Campbell posed no immediate threat to police before Frashour fatally shot him in the parking lot of a Northeast Portland apartment complex on Jan. 29, 2010. Reese testified that Frashour, who he fired in November 2010, didn't have a right to shoot Frashour. An arbitrator has ordered Frashour be rehired, but the city has refused, and has challenged the arbitrator's decision before the state Employment Relations Board.

"He never displayed a weapon. He didn't take any offensive action towards the officer," Reese said, of Campbell, in his sworn arbitration testimony in the Frashour firing. "We can't use force on him."

For Campbell to have posed an immediate threat, the chief testified, he would have had to take an "offensive action"—"turn toward us, pull something out, take a shooting stance."

The chief's testimony stunned Portland police rank-and-file officers, union leaders and the union's use-of-force expert, who say the chief articulated a new standard, one that's inconsistent with their training. And in the end, the arbitrator discounted the chief's stance in her March ruling, ordering Frashour be reinstated.

On Wednesday, in a prepared statement released by the bureau with the use of force report, Reese said, "The community has expressed concern over police use of force and we are hoping to highlight the enhancements the Police Bureau has made and show the use of force numbers have declined. We also want community members to know we review every use of force report and will continue to monitor the numbers."

Dan Handelman, of the police watchdog group Portland Copwatch, called the report "thin."

"It's interesting information, but I think it's too thin," said Handelman.

He said the report doesn't identify whether the use of less-lethal force is up or down or the number of police shootings has dropped. Handleman said police shootings since 2007 have increased in number, with two in 2007, four by 2011 and five or six so far this year, depending if you include the shooting by a Portland cop in Aloha earlier this year.

"This mostly looks like a fluff, PR piece," Handelman said. "We need more information to be able to have a meaningful discussion as a community."

UPDATE: […] Portland police Sgt. Pete Simpson released further data, which was not included in the report.

The new data not included in the report breaks down use of force incidents involving the pointing of firearms, takedowns, Tasers, control holds, police Hobble restraints, pepper spray, bean bag shotgun use and batons.

It shows that officers' pointing of firearms has dropped 37 percent from 2008 through 2011, from 813 incidents in 2008 to 509 in 2011. Police takedowns had a similar drop, from 539 in 2008 to 341 in 2011, a 37 percent drop.

Taser use dropped 40 percent, according to police data - from 378 incidents in 2008 to 228 in 2011, the data shows.

Yet, pepper spray use rose 21 percent between 2008 and 2011, from 58 incidents in 2008 to 70 cases in 2011, the new data released after the report shows.

Officer-involved shootings also have risen over the last several years, the requested data shows. The bureau data shows there were six officer-involved shootings in 2010, compared to one in 2009, two in 2008, two in 2007, five officer-involved shootings and two deaths in police custody in 2006.

The Oakland Police Are Turning Over a New Leaf

Joaquin Palomino

Joaquin Palomino is a data and investigative reporter at the San Francisco Chronicle. *He has also written for outlets like* National Geographic, *the Verge, Al Jazeera America, and Reuters.*

Excessive use of force has long been a problem for the Oakland Police Department, leading to civic distrust, costly lawsuits and the nation's longest-running federal intervention.

Despite several recent officer-involved shootings, a Chronicle analysis of Oakland Police Department data shows such incidents are becoming less common. Officer-involved shootings, excessive force complaints and incidents in which officers used force have all declined precipitously over the past three years in Oakland.

Save any major slipup, the department, which has been monitored by a federal court since 2003, is expected to soon regain its autonomy. It would save the city millions and help the law enforcement agency shed its reputation as one of America's most dysfunctional.

But if history is any indication, maintaining the gains achieved under federal oversight could be just as daunting as securing them.

"We have seen improvement, but the jury is still out on whether it will be sustainable," said civil rights attorney Jim Chanin, who has helped oversee the department's reforms. "There are some positive signs that it will be, but we don't know yet."

OPD by the numbers

The Oakland Police Department averaged roughly eight officer-involved shootings per year between 2000 and 2012. There have been just six over the past 24 months, including the uptick this summer—a decline of more than 60 percent in shootings from the prior decade's average.

Alameda County sheriff's deputies and Highway Patrol officers were involved in four shootings in Oakland over the same time frame, all of them fatal, despite having fewer cops on the streets, according to data obtained through a public records request.

A review of more than 22,000 use-of-force incidents also shows less severe altercations between police and the public are on the decline.

Between 2009 and 2014, the number of use-of-force incidents recorded by the department dropped four-fold, from 3,902 to 895. There were 49 incidents reported in July — the lowest monthly count in the reviewed time frame.

If current trends continue, aggressive interactions with the public would drop to 630 in 2015.

The falling numbers are a good indication that police-community relations are improving, according to Barry Krisberg, a UC Berkeley criminologist. "Oakland has been pretty quiet compared to the 600 bullets fired in Stockton, or some pretty horrendous lethal-force incidents in San Jose," he said.

Use-of-force complaints, which include a range of behaviors from grabbing suspects by the hair or bending their wrist to choke holds and shootings, also dipped more than 40 percent from 2013 through 2014. Grievances filed with the Citizens' Police Review Board—which investigates some excessive-force allegations — steadily declined from a high of 90 in 2009 to 15 in 2014.

Meanwhile, arrests have remained relatively steady, suggesting the positive numbers may not be the result of lax policing.

A long time coming

Along with improvements in community relations, certain crimes have also dropped. Homicides fell from 126 in 2012 to 80 in 2014. The numbers are on pace to be about the same this year. Serious crimes fell 8 percent over the same time period.

"We have had three successive years of double-digit reductions in shootings, so we're definitely having an impact," Oakland Police Chief Sean Whent said in an interview with The Chronicle. "But it's still a high-crime city and we have a lot more work to do."

The improvements have been a long time coming.

A handful of law enforcement agencies have struggled to complete federal mandates to reform, but none has been under oversight for longer than Oakland, which entered what is known as the Negotiated Settlement Agreement more than a decade ago.

Misconduct payouts

The department's difficulties have provoked ire from court-appointed monitors and some community members.

The frequency with which officers drew and pointed guns at suspects, the handling of the Occupy Oakland protests—which resulted in hefty misconduct settlements including a $4.5 million payment to an Iraq War veteran shot in the face with a tear gas canister—and inability of the department to punish bad cops were all regularly criticized by courts and city leaders.

Some feared the department would never turn a new leaf.

Things began to change, though, in 2013 after Whent was appointed chief. He ushered in new use-of-force trainings, updated foot and vehicle pursuit policies to keep officers out of dangerous situations and oversaw the full implementation of the body camera program—which has been attributed to improved interactions between police and civilians.

"Oakland needed fresh leadership and I think they got it," Krisberg said. "There's no reason to think that police-community relations, which had deteriorated so badly, could have fixed themselves."

Maintaining the gains

Oakland police still need to iron out some lingering suggestions from the federal monitors, including expanding the department's use-of-force review board, more thoroughly tracking vehicle-stop data and addressing the issue of fired cops being re-hired through arbitration. Still, the department and some civic leaders believe an end of federal oversight is on the horizon.

The prospect elicits both hope and anxiety.

"There is a long history of important reforms that, for one reason or another, simply faded away," said Samuel Walker, a criminologist at the University of Nebraska who has studied the OPD. "This has been a problem for the entire history of policing."

Anticorruption policies implemented at the New York Police Department in the 1970s helped clean up the force, but the reforms didn't last. In 1993, a special mayoral panel determined that NYPD "had failed at every level to uproot corruption," and that it "concealed lawlessness by police officers," according to the New York Times.

The San Diego Police Department exemplified best-practice policing throughout the 1980s and 1990s, Walker said, but it was recently rocked by a sexual assault scandal. Ten officers were investigated for rape, domestic violence, driving under the influence and sexual battery during a three-month span in 2011, according to a U.S. Department of Justice audit; six were ultimately arrested. More sexual assault cases piled up in 2014 and 2015.

"Community leaders in Oakland have to be diligent, they can't just say, 'The war is over,' " Walker said. "The department will be on its own, so it's up to Oakland to ensure that they don't slide back."

Some have proposed creating a police commission — a civilian board that sets policy and conducts disciplinary hearings for misconduct. In theory, a commission would add an extra layer of oversight if and when the monitors pack up.

An insurance policy

"After having spent so many millions of dollars and so much time, why would we not want to make sure there's a protection in place to keep us from losing our investment?" said Rashidah Grinage, former executive director of Oakland police watchdog group PUEBLO.

Whent thinks improvements can be cemented in without a commission.

He points to his department's 700 body cameras — roughly the same number as sworn officers — and the fact the city has set aside money for two new auditors at the Office of the Inspector General, which keeps tabs on the Police Department. He also said the department plans to make a civilian the head of internal affairs.

All should help keep the progress intact, he noted.

"That would be the biggest disaster; if we were to end the Negotiated Settlement Agreement and then all of the sudden go back to something else," Whent said. "It really is my goal that the day it ends, nobody recognizes any difference."

CHAPTER 4

Do We Need to Change the Way We Train Police?

Overview: Empathy Training May Lead to New Standards

Christopher Moraff

Christopher Moraff is a reporting fellow at John Jay College of Criminal Justice and frequently writes about policing, criminal justice policy, and civil liberties for outlets like Next City and the Daily Beast.

Yesterday, a grand jury refused to indict a member of the NYPD for asphyxiating asthmatic suspect Eric Garner in July with a "chokehold" maneuver banned by his department. In the past two weeks, a police officer in Cleveland whose record reflected he had "dismal" handgun skills gunned down a 12-year-old holding a BB gun in a Cleveland park, and autopsy results showed that a mentally ill man shot 14 times by a police officer in Milwaukee was hit in the back. In all three cases the police officer involved was white while the suspect was black.

These deaths once again press the need to address the way officers engage the public at large, and public mistrust that results from such examples is one of the reasons some police departments, from Washington state to Chicago, are making an effort to put "protect and serve" back at the forefront of policing. Philadelphia Police Commissioner Charles Ramsey might want to look to how both are taking the lead. Earlier this week, President Obama appointed Ramsey head of a national Task Force on 21st Century Policing, as part of an initiative to address the breakdown in police-community relations that has taken over the public dialogue since the August shooting of 18-year-old Mike Brown by an officer in Ferguson, Missouri.

In an interview with the Associated Press, Chief Ramsey called the task ahead of him "daunting, but … doable."

"Can Different Training Make Police Officers Guardians, Not Warriors?" by Christopher Moraff, Nextcity, December 4, 2014. Reprinted by Permission.

Revising Police Training

In 2012, Chicago tapped a team of Yale criminologists to remodel its officer training program under a mandate from Police Superintendent Garry F. McCarthy. By January 2014, more than 8,000 Police Academy graduates had been schooled in the new curriculum—which teaches officers to be responsive, impartial, respectful and fair.

Proponents of the strategy say it not only reduces tensions between police and the community, but improves public safety by making citizens more likely to obey laws and cooperate with police.

Members of Chicago's Police Education and Training Division spent the spring and summer retraining officers in the California cities of Salinas, Oakland and Stockton and are now fanning out to other municipalities to share what they learned.

Exactly one year after Chicago finalized its new curriculum, Washington graduated its first class of police recruits through a radically modified officer training program. The goal is to put police on the street who can navigate tense situations with empathy while respecting the impact their actions have on how situations unfold.

The training strategy is the brainchild of Sue Rahr, who left her job as sheriff of King County to take over as head of the Washington State Criminal Justice Training Commission in 2012. David Bales, Rahr's deputy, says the program dispenses with military-style boot-camp elements common to many police academies in favor of coursework focused on communication and conflict resolution. In addition to traditional training in firearms and takedown techniques, recruits take courses in behavioral psychology and are encouraged to talk problems out rather than simply respond to barked orders.

"We are guided by the underlying goal of producing officers who are guardians as opposed to warriors," says Bales, who himself has more than three decades of law enforcement experience.

"The most common corresponding emotion to fear is anger, and anger does not facilitate ongoing compliance," he adds. "We teach recruits that when they mistreat people they actually may make that person more dangerous."

The program is hardly a cakewalk. In one exercise, described in an article published last year in the Seattle Times, recruits are doused twice in the face with pepper spray and asked to complete a series of tasks that frequently includes reciting the federal and state statutes governing the use of force.

Bales says the purpose of the exercise is to demonstrate to officers that they can focus, think, problem solve, defend themselves and even deescalate while under extreme duress.

"When an officer has confidence in their abilities, they are less likely to overreact out of fear," he says.

Unintended Consequences

Despite a pronounced drop in crime, technological improvements in policing and the increased professionalism of law enforcement, surveys show that "trust and confidence" in police has remained relatively unchanged (averaging about 50 percent) for four decades. New polling from Gallup shows that whites are significantly more likely to express trust in police than blacks.

At least part of the problem can be viewed as an unintended consequence of the war on drugs—which turned entire communities into de facto battlefields and a generation of young men of color into potential enemy combatants.

Reining in police militarization (another goal of the Obama administration's new proposal) is a vital first step to repairing the damage. But even the most deadly weapon is just a mindless tool. It's the attitude and character of the police officer holding it that matters.

In a statement provided to Next City, Chief Ramsey acknowledged the importance of officer behavior in informing the overall tone of police-community relations: "We as police departments have an obligation to build public trust and that starts with transparent behavior and developing police legitimacy across the board."

A report released last March by the Police Executive Research Forum, which Ramsey heads, also highlighted the critical role police "legitimacy" and the related concept of "procedural justice" play in effective law enforcement. The latter concept refers to the belief, supported by decades of scholarly research, that processes that are perceived to be fair are the most likely to generate favorable outcomes.

Criminologists such as Yale's Tom Tyler, who has spent decades studying the effect of officer behavior on law abidance, have found that citizens are more likely to gauge their interactions with police based on the perceived fairness of law enforcement rather than its effectiveness or lawfulness.

"The issue of interpersonal treatment consistently emerges as a key factor in reactions to dealings with legal authorities," Tyler writes. "[P]eople focus on cues that communicate information about the intentions and character of the legal authorities with whom they are dealing."

For instance, he cites studies that suggest members of minority groups factor how they are treated by police into determining whether they have been racially profiled. (This helps explain why policies like stop-and-frisk tend to be counterproductive).

Fewer Deadly Encounters

It hardly needs to be said that not shooting people who don't deserve to be shot is a crucial piece of the police legitimacy puzzle. Calling a shooting justified is not the same thing as calling it necessary; this has led some departments to rethink the way they train their officers in the use of deadly force.

Following the police shooting in Albuquerque last March of homeless camper James Boyd, the New Mexico Law Enforcement Academy began instructing officers to take cover and consider their options instead of immediately engaging aggressive suspects.

Two months earlier, Dallas Police Chief David O. Brown issued changes to the department's use-of-force program to require training once every quarter instead of bi-annually.

In the wake of the Mike Brown shooting, one city, Richmond, California, emerged as the poster child for the police reform movement for going five years without a single fatal shooting by its officers despite the city's long history of violent crime. Richmond Police Chief Chris Magnus credits the achievement to the expanded use of non-lethal weapons and monthly firearms training focused on accuracy and accountability.

Over the last five years, the Richmond PD has expended just eight bullets on five people. That's nearly as many bullets that Officer Darren Wilson fired into Mike Brown. (It's worth noting that Wilson's grand jury testimony also suggests that Ferguson police are given the discretion over whether to carry non-lethal weapons such as Tasers.)

On September 14th, Richmond experienced its first fatal officer involved shooting since 2007, to which the city responded with two separate investigations and a concerted community outreach effort. Both the police chief and his deputy attended the victim's funeral in civilian clothes to avoid provocation.

Chief Magnus's ability to think empathetically about his impact on the community he serves has won him high praise both inside and outside of Richmond. In September, he was summoned to Ferguson as one of two law enforcement experts tapped by the DOJ to review civil rights charges in connection with the Mike Brown killing.

As they move forward with their mission it's fair to say the members of the President's new trust-building task force can learn a lot from the experiences of forward-thinking leaders like Magnus.

The Washington State Criminal Justice Training Commission is now working with Seattle University to gauge if the department's new empathy training is having its intended effect. Deputy Director Bales says that while it may be too soon for any concrete evidence, there's no doubt in his mind that he is helping put better, more responsive police officers of the streets of his state.

"Empathy connects us to people, makes us better crisis interventionists, better investigators, better public servants and healthier, happier people," he says. "Could it be a national model? I don't know, but we will enthusiastically contribute to the discussion and the development of best practice in any way we can."

Inadequate Training Can Only Lead to Trouble

Paul Waldman

Paul Waldman is a senior writer for the American Prospect as well as a writer for the Plum Line blog at the Washington Post *and a columnist for the* Week. *He's also a published author.*

Maria Haberfeld is a professor at the John Jay College of Criminal Justice in New York. A veteran of the Israel Defense Forces who also served in the Israel National Police, she has conducted research on police forces in multiple countries, and has also written many books on terrorism and policing, including Critical Issues in Police Training. We spoke on Friday about the events in Ferguson, Missouri, and the shooting of Kajieme Powell by St. Louis police, which was caught on video. Powell, brandishing a steak knife, approached officers, saying "Shoot me!" As reported by the Post-Dispatch, St. Louis Police Chief Sam Dotson said lethal force was permitted under department rules if a knife-wielding attacker is within 21 feet of police.

Paul Waldman: Did you think what the officers did [in Powell's shooting] was appropriate? It seems pretty clear that that's standard operating procedure.

Maria Haberfeld: Yes it is, absolutely.

PW: Are those procedures adequate to deal with those kinds of situations?

MH: The procedures are adequate; what's not adequate is the way police officers are trained. That's the problem, and this is something

I've been talking about for decades. The majority of police officers are overwhelmingly trained with a focus on the technical part of use of force, and are not trained enough in the emotional, psychological, physiological aspects of use of force. And of course, the social aspects of use of force: how this all plays later on within the community, how it impacts police-community relations.

So the use of force is not something that should stand alone. Unfortunately, in most of the training academies, it does stand alone, even if there is some rhetoric about, "Oh yes, we integrate [it] into other modules." The reality is—and I look at police training all the time, in various jurisdictions around the country and around the world—that's not the case, unfortunately.

PW: So, is most of [that training] focused on "Here's how to protect ourselves"? It seems that's the message when you hear police representatives talk about this. Their focus is, obviously, that police work is very dangerous, and if there's any kind of a threat at all, we're going to neutralize it.

MH: Yes, but how you perceive the threat is a subjective thing, and how you go about neutralizing the threat is also a subjective thing, even though they're trained around this continuum of force that allows them to go from one step to another, or skip a number of stages based on their assessment of the situation. Their assessment of the situation sometimes can be exaggerated based on their previous experience, based on what's going on in any given moment, based on the bystanders' reactions. So it's a very complicated and complex issue that cannot be just explained by: "We have the right, we are authorized, and it's our discretion."

There are a host of variables that go into things. And those variables, at least in my mind, should be constantly addressed, and not end with the police officer graduating from police academy, and then the only thing they have to do is to qualify twice a year whether or not they can still carry a weapon. But this qualifying twice a year is focused completely on the technical aspect of use of deadly force.

PW: One thing I've seen in the discussions about this is, for instance, that the police in England and Wales fire their guns only a few times in a year.

MH: Because they're not armed.

PW: So that raises a couple of questions. If most of them are not armed, what do those police do if they don't have guns, and they're confronted with a suspect who, say, has a knife?

MH: First of all, there are a few countries where police forces are not armed—Ireland would be the other one. The British police have units that are armed, and if there is a situation that would require an armed backup, then the backup is called for. But a situation like this, where they have somebody with a knife, it's a simple explanation. It goes back to training. Police forces in the U.K., in Ireland, in other countries where police forces are not armed, they have a much more extensive, in-depth training than we have. An average training in the United States is fifteen weeks. Fifteen weeks is nothing. Police forces in other countries have twice, three times as long training as we have here.

It's all about how police officers are prepared to deal with people who pose threats to them or to others. This is not something that we should save money on, but to me, that's exactly what we're doing. We are saving money on police training, saying that it's very expensive to have longer training. And I think it's irresponsible in a democratic society to say that a profession that has the authority to use deadly force, we just should shorten the training because a longer training is too expensive. Basically, what we're doing is putting a dollar sign on people's lives, both police officers and members of the public.

PW: So that means that if you're a policeman someplace else—

England, France, Germany—you're going to be trained so that you're better capable of talking that person down and getting them to put down their knife or their pipe or whatever it is that they have?

MH: No doubt in my mind, based on what I am seeing in police training in other countries, that police officers are better prepared to deal with the public over there than the ones we have here. No doubt in my mind, based on the research that I have done over the years.

PW: Do you think that a controversy like this one will make police forces around the country more likely to reexamine how they do their training?

MH: No.

PW: It won't make any difference at all?

MH: No, and I'll tell you why. Ninety percent of the police budget goes to salaries in any department. So, whatever is left is allocated to equipment and some other stuff, and nothing is left for training. The majority of police departments around the country don't have in-service training. So if you don't have the money, you're not going to re-examine.

PW: Well that's a little depressing.

MH: It is depressing. I've been writing about this for twenty years, it's very depressing to me. [Most] police departments in the United States are not NYPD or LAPD. Police departments in the United States are exactly what we're seeing—the Ferguson police department, fifty cops. This is the average size of a police department in the United States. So you can understand that a department of that size is not going to get any resources. This is very sad, and this is why I've been talking about the need to centralize law enforcement in the United States, to professionalize their response to the public, not just about use of force, but about everything.

Because policing is not just about the high-profile incidents, it's also about how they perform on a daily basis vis-à-vis the public. But this requires skills, this requires education, this requires training. An average police department, all they care about is whether you have a GED, and you didn't use drugs in the last three years. I mean, it's ridiculous. If somebody looks at this a little bit closer, then it's really scary.

PW: Is the training and the resulting way the cops deal with the public—not just about the use of force but about everything—do you think that is superior in other Western countries, too?

MH: Absolutely. I don't think, I know, because I do research with police departments in other countries, I see their training, I visit the departments, their police academies. That's what I've been doing for almost twenty years, so I know exactly that it's superior over there—not in each and every country, but the majority of police forces in democratic countries today—yes, absolutely.

Police Reform Is the Key to the Future

Norm Stamper

Norm Stamper is the former Seattle police chief, serving from 1994 to 2000. He has since authored a book about the dark side of policing.

*F*ormer Seattle Police Chief Norm Stamper knows what it is like to be at the center of a firestorm over police conduct. In 2000, when the World Trade Organization convention took over his city, Stamper's officers were criticized for their heavy-handed, and often violent, response to street protests.

Hundreds of peaceful protesters were arrested and rounded up along with those who had smashed store windows and destroyed police cars. Stamper resigned that year.

Since his resignation, Stamper has become a vocal proponent of police reform. Last month, he published "To Protect and Serve: How to Fix America's Police," which outlines his vision of police forces trained to meet national standards, gleaned from more than three decades of experience in the uniform.

Stamper says police shootings, like those of Alton Sterling and Philando Castile, are further evidence that change is urgently needed. He says the prevalence of guns in American society contributes to the distrust that has grown between the police and the communities they patrol—a point President Barack Obama addressed this weekend, speaking in response to the fatal shooting of five Dallas police officers.

Here is Stamper in his own words, as told to Kerry Shaw of The Trace.

When I heard about Dallas, I felt heartsick. I don't have a television, but I'm online a lot, and the alerts started pouring in. These were police officers, selected for the color of their skin.

The other thing that went through my mind was that this will be a huge setback to Black Lives Matter. A number of police officers

"I Ran a Big City Police Department. The Way We Train Cops to Use Lethal Force Is Broken," by Norm Stamper, The Trace, July 12, 2016. Reprinted by Permission.

around the country have been condemning the movement for months. I've even seen links from various police groups talking about how disgusting it is. They've countered with Blue Lives Matter, and that is a movement now.

So what we have is polarization, and polarization is never good. It's worse now than it was before the Dallas shootings.

I was also concerned that the shootings by police that happened before Thursday night's assassinations would get lost, and that as a country we'd forget that people are hurting and it's not just cops.

As we watch these shootings unfold, repeatedly, on a dashcam of a police car or an iPhone video, we're left with the impression that police officers do not—and this is a sweeping generalization—place sanctity on human life. They're too quick to pull the trigger. We've seen too many [shootings] that didn't have to happen, where there was minimal risk to the officer. That's causing enormous anger and terrible sadness in the African-American community and other segments of our society. Many cops are also disturbed by this, but they don't speak out as much as they should.

The Supreme Court has made it very clear that the only time a police officer can use lethal force is when your life or the life of another is at imminent risk. We have 18,000 law enforcement agencies. That's 18,000 different policies for determining imminent risk, 18,000 different sets of procedures and tactics. The room for different interpretations, even within a police station, is substantial.

Wouldn't it be nice if every cop and every citizen could know what the actual practice was for lethal force? Or for stop-and-frisk or search-and-seizure? When it comes to stopping an American on the streets, or when it comes time to pull a gun or a trigger, the standards need to be the same from coast to coast.

Right now we don't have any national standards for policing. Instead we have a patchwork of policies, with wide variation in training, supervision, and performance evaluation. I think the average citizen would be surprised to know how unsupervised one of the most delicate and dangerous jobs is.

The process of setting and enforcing the standards should be done at the federal level in conjunction with local agencies. Each agency needs to have sufficient muscle to say, "We'll certify every cop, we'll certify every agency. Oh and by the way, in extreme situations, we'll de-certify any cop or agency."

If you get de-certified as a police officer, don't even think about applying across town. You've forfeited your right to be a police officer.

In creating those standards, we'd have to reach some consistency in training. Now we typically provide many hours of firearms training but very few hours of training in de-escalation. Since Ferguson, some agencies have really bolstered their training in de-escalation, but many have not. Some are full-blown military stress academies.

If you want police officers to act like soldiers — and I'd hope that we don't, but rather as true domestic peacekeepers, partnered with their communities — then the last thing you'd do is train them under a militaristic model.

An academy should pose challenges, but those ought to be structured simulations of what police officers encounter in the real world — people pulling guns on you, knives on you, calling you names. You want police officers to be self-confident people.

We can also dramatically improve training so that a cop can understand how his body reacts in a stressful, ambiguous situation: like when there may be a gun, or when a baby has entered the scene at the same time as a gun. These are shoot/don't shoot scenarios that are likely to occur on the job. Right now we do these simulations once in training. Maybe we bring someone in a second time if they made questionable choices.

Of course, guns play a big role in all this. They put another level of pressure on police officers. Guns make it all the more evident that the next domestic violence incident or bar room brawl could have someone packing heat. Guns make police officers hyper vigilant. And a scared cop is a dangerous cop.

Fear, more than anything, distorts perception. It causes individuals to see things that aren't there. It can cause them to experience tunnel vision. They'll focus on the threat at the expense sometimes of everything around it. Often tunnel vision will not allow you to see an innocent bystander. It will not allow you to recognize that you have an opportunity to take cover, that you don't have to stand there, exposed to someone with a gun.

I am extremely disturbed by the proliferation of guns in the country, and most major city chiefs feel the same way I do.

We need true community policing. I'm envisioning a system where citizens are invited to participate in hiring and instructing new police officers. They'd also be involved in police oversight. (I avoid using the word "civilians," as it creates the mindset that police officers are soldiers.)

And, finally, we have to find a way to end the drug war. By definition, you don't fight a war without enemies. And that's what we're doing, and we're targeting people of color in wildly disproportionate numbers. And then we wonder why there's such a strain on the relationships between cops and young black men.

And you could say, "Oh, they're breaking the law." Well, so are young white men. But black men are being targeted at disproportionately higher rates.

We know prohibition didn't work, and that was very similar to the war we're now waging against illegal drugs. We've spent $1.3 trillion since Nixon declared drugs "public enemy number one" and we have incarcerated tens of millions of people—that number needs to sink in—for nonviolent drug offenses. And what do we have to show for it? Drugs are more available, more potent, and more accessible to our children. It's been a colossal failure.

Police Power Can Be a Dangerous Thing

David Rudovsky

David Rudovsky is a senior fellow at the University of Pennsylvania Law School. He teaches courses in evidence, criminal law, and criminal procedure.

As a result of recent high-profile shootings of unarmed African American civilians by police, the long simmering problem of excessive police force in the United States has sparked a national debate on policing, race, and community relations. As has been the case on repeated occasions in our nation's history, claims of unlawful or oppressive police practices have focused attention on the powers granted to law enforcement, the use of these powers against racial minorities, political activists, dissidents, and others who challenge the status quo, and on the appropriate remedial mechanisms. And although the great majority of interactions between police and civilians do not involve force or unreasonable force, video-documented incidents of excessive force have moved the debate from one of "is there a problem" to the scope of excessive force, its causes, and effective remedies.

Data collection is still inexcusably deficient in many police agencies, but the data that are available demonstrate patterns of excessive force, as well as large racial disparities in the use of force. A recent study on racial and ethnic disparities in the use of lethal police force from the years 2010 to 2014, by Dr. James W. Buehler of Drexel University, reported 2,285 deaths that resulted from police use of force. The same study found that among males who were 10 years and older, the mortality rate for African Americans and Latinos was 2.8 and 1.7 times higher respectively when compared with Whites.

Other studies have shown significantly higher rates of shootings among unarmed African Americans when compared

"The Troubling Issues Regarding Police Use of Force," by David Rudovsky, University of Pennsylvania Law School, February 27, 2017. Reprinted by Permission.

with Whites. In Philadelphia—a city that has approximately 45 percent White, 44 percent African American, and 14 percent Latino residents—80 percent of force incidents involved African-American suspects, 10 percent involved Latinos, and 9 percent involved Whites.

To be sure, more must be considered before these data can be said to show a causal relationship based on race, since other factors—such as crime rates or the dangers inherent in different suspects' reactions to police intervention—might explain the racial disparities. However, in related studies involving incarceration rates and stop-and-frisk encounters, non-racial factors have not explained similarly large racial disparities. For example, in litigation surrounding Philadelphia's stop-and-frisk practices— where the racial data were quite similar to the data on use of force—regression studies have shown that factors such as crime rates, police deployment, and social or economic conditions do not explain the racial differentials in stop-and-frisk practices.

The debate over the causes of unlawful or unreasonable police use of force has focused on the role of (1) law enforcement agencies, in terms of training, supervision, and discipline of officers; in short, on the critical issue of agency and individual accountability, (2) the courts, in terms of remedies that are (or are not) available for excessive force, both to compensate individuals whose rights have been violated and to create a system of remedial measures that have a deterrent effect, (3) civilian review agencies, and the powers of investigation and discipline that should be vested in them, and (4) prosecutors, who have the power to bring criminal prosecutions against officers who engage in the criminal use of force.

Over the years, commentators have documented systemic deficiencies in each of these agencies in controlling and remedying excessive force. In my view, although there is a need for civilian review, litigation involving systemic deficiencies in police policies and practices, and robust judicial oversight, the primary responsibility for developing practices and policies that can ensure effective, equitable, and reasonable uses of force lies with law enforcement agencies. If police departments do not address and "own" the problem, oversight by prosecutors, civilian review boards, and the courts will not provide sufficient counterweights.

Other commentators in this series have shown the reasons why criminal prosecutions, civil rights litigation, and court interventions have not been effective in controlling police violence. Criminal prosecutions are extremely rare as prosecutors must rely on police for the investigation of criminal cases and are reluctant to prosecute officers unless there is overwhelming evidence of serious misconduct. And juries often fail to convict even when the evidence is strong. Civilian review agencies are almost always without sufficient investigative, adjudicative, and disciplinary powers to effectuate departmental changes.

As for judicial intervention, the U.S. Supreme Court, through an application of a series of "judicial door closing" doctrines, has erected numerous roadblocks to effective civil rights litigation. The Court has given an extraordinarily high level of deference to officers who employ force and has interpreted the Fourth Amendment in a manner that only prohibits the most egregious use of force. As Professors Brandon Garrett and Seth Stoughton have commented, "Fourth Amendment case law is not only poorly suited for police training, but [is] actually counterproductive."

Further, the doctrine of qualified immunity protects officers from damage actions even when their actions have violated the Fourth Amendment, injunctive relief is often barred by standing principles, and except in cases of clear systemic violations of constitutional protections, police departments, municipalities, and states are immune from suit. Although some litigation reform efforts have succeeded—in particular, interventions by the U.S. Department of Justice (DOJ) Civil Rights Division—these initiatives may be in jeopardy with the change in administrations.

So, what is to be done? First and foremost, as Jonathan Smith, the former Chief of the Special Litigation Section of the Civil Rights Division of the DOJ, and others have written, real reform is not possible without the democratization of policing through community participation among those most affected by policing tactics and enhanced transparency in operations. In many ways the police are the least regulated arm of government, notwithstanding their enormous powers. Administrative law principles could be used to require a democratic process of adoption of rules and regulations that control and limit departmental use of force.

Second, police departments must engage in an in-depth review of use-of-force policies and training. For the past 50 years, with the advent of proactive policing characterized by "zero tolerance practices," aggressive stop-and-frisk policies, and a militarization of police forces, the "warrior" model of policing has become dominant.

However, with the recent attention to excessive force and racial bias, a new debate has emerged, spurred in part by the Black Lives Matter movement. In 2016, the Police Executive Research Forum, a national organization of police officials, issued recommendations on use of force that provide a "guardian" model for policing. These principles stress respect for the sanctity of human life, the need for standards for the use of force that are more restrictive than those imposed by the Constitution, force that is proportional to the dangers of the situation, de-escalation techniques, and fair, transparent, and independent investigations of the use of force.

These and other related recommendations were also made by President Barack Obama's Task Force on 21st Century Policing. The task force emphasized comprehensive data collection as a means towards greater transparency in operations, prioritizing de-escalation tactics, diversity in police ranks, internal accountability, and strong action on racial profiling. These recommendations mirror many of the provisions of consent decrees initiated by the DOJ in its investigative and litigation efforts under its "pattern or practice" authority.

Third, police training must accentuate the need for officers to refrain from escalating tactics and to develop communication and other related skills that can reduce incidents of deadly and other kinds of serious force. Many use-of-force incidents involve mentally ill persons who pose a danger only to themselves. The

Washington Post has reported that 25 percent of all fatal shootings by police are of persons suffering from serious mental illness. Police departments should establish "Crisis Intervention Teams" that are trained to respond to these incidents with tactics of patience, deliberation, and de-escalation.

Further, police policies must go beyond the highly deferential constitutional standards announced by the Supreme Court. In a recent case, San Francisco v. Sheehan, the Supreme Court missed the opportunity to adjust constitutional standards to the realities of police use of deadly force. The Court granted qualified immunity to an officer who responded to a report of a mentally disabled woman living in a group home who was threatening to hurt herself with a knife by making an unannounced intrusion into the room in which she was located. When she responded, not surprisingly, by moving towards him with the knife, he fired several times.

Notwithstanding universal agreement among policing and psychology experts that an officer in these encounters should not enter barricaded rooms and that trained negotiators should be called to de-escalate the tension, the Court determined that no clearly established Fourth Amendment rights had been violated because the officer faced the threat of serious bodily injury when he used deadly force. But if "reasonableness" is the touchstone of the Fourth Amendment, why would the Court credit the decision to use deadly force as one made in a "split-second" context and ignore the officer's responsibility in creating the danger?

Fourth, officers should be provided with less-than-lethal equipment such as safe chemical sprays and electronic control weapons like tasers—along with comprehensive training and supervision—that can be used when resistance is serious but not life-threatening, and the suspect can be safely secured without deadly force.

Fifth, to ensure proper accountability, internal investigations must be conducted with integrity, provide appropriate discipline and retraining when fault has been found, and implement a high level of transparency surrounding investigative information and decision-making. Investigators must also recognize the deleterious effects of the police "code of silence" on their adjudications. All too often, lack of accountability leads the offender and other officers to assume that breaking the rules has no consequences.

Sixth, departments must expand the use of technology that promotes accountability and transparency. Many of the recent controversial use-of-force incidents became known only through police body-worn and surveillance cameras, as well as cell phone videos. All departments should be moving to universal body and patrol car cameras, with regulations that require that these cameras function at all critical stages of police-civilian interactions.

Seventh, more attention must be paid to explicit and implicit racial bias. This concern cuts across hiring, training, and supervision of officers and should incorporate the new advances and learning with respect to the phenomenon of "implicit bias," which relates to how unconscious attitudes and perceptions may alter a person's view and understanding of other people's conduct and actions. For police, this is especially important in their assessment of the dangers posed by civilians, and in particular suspects who may pose a risk of physical danger to the officer.

There is experiential evidence of the effectiveness of new paradigms and cultures of policing. For example, due to concerns about the levels and patterns of force by officers in the Philadelphia Police Department, former Philadelphia Police Commissioner Charles Ramsey requested a study by the DOJ on the Police Department's policies, training, and investigations of use of force. The study produced a wide-ranging set of recommendations that were soon implemented by the Philadelphia Police Department. More time will be required before definitive conclusions can be drawn, but it is instructive that use-of-force patterns in Philadelphia appear to have changed in significant ways. Thus, comparing data from 2012 with 2015, the Philadelphia Police Department reported the following:

	2012	2015
NUMBER OF POLICE SHOOTING INCIDENTS	59	35
NUMBER OF SHOTS FIRED AT CIVILIANS	477	200
PERSONS KILLED BY POLICE	16	2
PERSONS INJURED BY POLICE	32	15
NUMBER OF OFFICERS FIRING AT PERSONS	104	46

The renewed debate on police use of force provides an opportunity to correct both the constitutional and operational standards in an area that poses fundamental challenges to our commitment to restraints on necessary—but widely abused—governmental powers.

De-Escalation in Dallas Is Paying Off

Naomi Martin

Naomi Martin is a staff writer at the Dallas Morning News, *where she covers government and politics. She has also covered the police in Dallas, New Orleans, and Baton Rouge.*

In a vacant school last week, two Dallas officers—one with a gun, the other a Taser—tried to talk a hulking man out of shooting himself.

The man left his guns behind and walked toward them. Stop, the cops said. He didn't.

"I'm going less lethal," an officer said. He fired his Taser.

Commanders said the outcome of the encounter, which was a staged police training drill, marked a vast change from old-school policing. They said in years past, that type of situation could've ended in a chokehold or a shooting.

Police Chief David Brown says this shift toward de-escalation is driving a sharp drop in excessive-force complaints against officers. In 2009, the year before Brown became chief, 147 such complaints were filed. So far this year, 13 have been filed—on pace to be the lowest number in at least two decades.

"This is the most dramatic development in policing anywhere in the country," Brown said in an interview Friday with The Dallas Morning News. "We've had this kind of impact basically through training, community policing and holding officers accountable."

Brown says his commanders have improved the quality of so-called reality-based training and increased required training hours for street cops over the past year. Trainers model the scenarios on real-life events recorded by officers' body cams, dash-cams, and the media.

"Dallas Police Excessive-Force Complaints Drop Dramatically," by Naomi Martin, Dallas Morning News Inc, November 2015. Reprinted by Permission.

"We can learn from what Dallas is doing," said Chuck Wexler, executive director of the Police Executive Research Forum in Washington, D.C. "That's what police departments need—they don't need training in silos: one day about the law, one day about firearms, one day about crisis intervention."

Brown believes the Dallas training has also led to a 30 percent decline in assaults on officers this year, and a 40 percent drop in shootings by police.

Slowing things down

Training instructors say they preach tactics that sometimes seem counter-intuitive to veteran officers: Slow down instead of rushing into a situation; don't approach a suspect immediately. Try to build a rapport; don't have multiple officers shout at once.

"By slowing things down, we're able to make better decisions and get more peaceful resolutions," said instructor Sgt. Anthony Greer.

Department leaders acknowledge that other factors also probably contributed to the decline in complaints, such as community engagement efforts. Also, the complaint decline coincides with street officers being outfitted with body microphones and dash-cam videos.

"The officers know they're being monitored," said Assistant Chief Tammie Hughes, who oversees internal affairs.

Excessive-force complaints have also dropped in Seattle, Birmingham, Baltimore, Portland, Ore., Paterson, N.J., and New York City.

The Dallas decline, though, seems to be among the most dramatic. The complaints dropped by 64 percent from 2009 to 2014.

Brown noted, however, that many uses of force by police are inevitable for officers to protect themselves.

Last year, two of 53 excessive-force complaints were sustained. One of those officers was fired. None of the 13 complaints filed so far this year have been sustained by investigators.

Skepticism

Several criminologists acknowledged that they were surprised by the drop in Dallas complaints, and said they would like to know more about how that happened.

"Anybody in any criminal justice research is going to be taken aback by such a dramatic swing in numbers," said Ronal Serpas, a former New Orleans police chief who is now a professor at Loyola University. But, he added, changes in training, accountability measures, and body microphones could have plausibly made a dent. "It could very well be true."

Without a formal study, there's no way to know for sure what caused the reduction in complaints, said John Worrall, a criminal justice professor at the University of Texas at Dallas.

"The marked drop between 2014 and 2015 strikes me as conspicuous and in need of an explanation," Worrall said. He said the chief's claim of training improvements could be valid, but added that "it is doubtful that such improvements could have such a pronounced effect in such a short span of time."

Alex Piquero, a fellow criminal justice professor at the university, said the complaint numbers could have also been affected by lower crime rates, citizens complaining less, and officers using less force.

Regardless, he said, the numbers appear to show a real change rather than just a random blip, because the trend "continues to go in the same direction for a sustained period of time."

But some critics expressed skepticism about Brown and his command staff's claims.

Slower 911 response times have much more to do with the drop than changes in training, which are a "smokescreen," said Ron Pinkston, president of the Dallas Police Association.

"We're not getting there in a timely manner, so the bad guys are already gone," Pinkston said. "The only complaint out there is the citizen saying, 'What took you so long?'"

Others said the reduction reflects a growing public opinion that filing a complaint is pointless.

"People don't feel that their complaints will be taken seriously, and they're right," said community activist John Fullinwider, co-founder of Mothers Against Police Brutality.

Teaching vs. testing

Reality-based training isn't new at the department, but Brown says the training has been ramped up in frequency and quality.

Officers on patrol, who respond to emergencies and therefore are most likely to use force on suspects, must complete the training every year now—twice as frequently as they used to go.

Deputy Chief Jeff Cotner, who now supervises the academy, says all patrol officers have been through the new classes. Records obtained by the *News* confirmed that a significant portion of all officers have cycled through the training in the past two years.

The academy's approach to training has changed, too, from a "testing" approach to a "teaching" one, said Executive Assistant Chief David Pughes, who oversaw reforms there last year. The scenarios now are more realistic, he said.

"You can have a reality-based training program all day long," Pughes said. "But if you're throwing people into unrealistic, no-win scenarios, you're not doing a whole lot to improve things."

Before the Ferguson, Mo., protests and unrest last year, Pughes said, much of American police training was geared toward responding to mass shootings. Officers were trained to rush ahead, find the shooter, and stop the threat to human lives immediately, which most of the time meant killing the shooter.

After Ferguson, departments rushed to add de-escalation, and Dallas beefed up its program, he said.

The training, which is held now at the old Lamar Elementary School, requires some imagination. The department is now trying to secure funding for a roughly $3 million to $4 million fake village with a gas station, school, apartment complex, and house.

"We definitely want our officers to defend themselves and we want them to go home at night," Brown said. "But we also want to avoid the controversies of a shooting that violates our deadly force policy. You do that through training."

"The Ferguson effect"

Another factor contributing to fewer force complaints could be what some law enforcement leaders call "the Ferguson effect"—the idea that officers are less likely now to confront suspects or use force because they don't want to risk being at the center of a viral incident.

But that notion is controversial among police officials. Many, including Brown, are insulted at the notion that officers would somehow abandon their duties in any way.

"Officers are still working hard and still doing their job," said Cotner. "I hear them [on the police radio] making themselves available and going toward the problem. You can't say ... there's a chilling effect."

Communities Need to Be Trained, Too

Andrew Bell & Bruce Razey

Andrew Bell has more than twenty years of experience in law enforcement and twenty-five years of experience in the US military and civilian service. He's now a criminal justice faculty member with American Military University. Bruce Razey enjoyed a thirty-year career in law enforcement, with one of his main jobs being police training.

In my 20-year police career, I [Bell] never discharged my weapon in the line of duty. However, there were several situations where I had legal justification to use a firearm, but, fortunately, my police training helped me find an alternative way to de-escalate the situation.

One such situation occurred when I was a young officer in the early 1980s. The call was to break up a high school fight. When I arrived at the scene, I pushed my way through a crowd of kids just in time to see one kid running away. When he got about 50 yards away, he turned around and came back to fight. I heard someone yell, "He's got a knife." As the 17-year-old got within about 30 yards, I could see a big butcher knife in his hand. He was now in a full sprint toward me.

When he was about 15 yards away, he started to raise the butcher knife. I still had my side-handle baton in my right hand. I dropped the baton on the ground and drew my weapon. I raised my weapon, formed a good sight picture on the kid's chest and started to pull the trigger. I thought I would cam the gun until the hammer fell. Camming is the ability to squeeze the trigger on a revolver and knowing the point where the hammer will fall striking the firing pin.

As I squeezed the trigger, my vision narrowed, sound was muffled and it seemed like time played in slow motion. Out of

"An Officer's Experience: Police Training to Reduce Use of Force Cases," by Andrew Bell and Bruce Razey, InPublicSafety.com, June 8, 2016. Reprinted by Permission.

my peripheral vision, I caught a glimpse of another kid holding my side-handle baton challenging the kid with the knife to fight. Suddenly, things seemed different. In an instant, I realized the kid with the knife was not trying to stab me, he was going after the other kid. I realized I could still take control of this without shooting, but I had to act quickly.

I holstered my revolver. Instantly, I was back in real time. I grabbed my baton away from the one kid and as I did the kid with the knife stopped dead (figuratively) in his tracks about five yards away. I looked at the kid with the knife and said, "Drop the knife." The kid threw the knife on the ground and ran in the opposite direction. Both kids were eventually apprehended and charged with disorderly conduct.

In those days, appropriate "less than lethal" weapon choices did not exist. The side-handle baton usually fell off your belt every time you ran and CS gas was seldom, if ever, used because innocent people nearby were often hit with the overspray. It wouldn't be until the late '80s and '90s when tools like the Taser, pepper spray and beanbag rounds came into play. Even then, not every officer had them.

The Importance of Combat Police Training

The only thing that stopped me from shooting that day was the combat police training I received as a young officer. Combat training is being aware of and understanding your environment and taking action based on changes to the situation. No advancements in technology or new less-than-lethal weapons will ever replace the value of combat training in teaching officers to recognize the threat and take the appropriate action. It is often the lack of proper police training and the lack of reality-based training that leads to escalation of force and unnecessary death.

Police departments across our nation spend a great deal of time and effort training their personnel to recognize when deadly force is authorized and legal. This is the proper thing to do, since departments and their employing municipalities are civilly liable for the actions of their officers. However, police departments should not stop there. In addition to honing firearms skills, marksmanship, and "shoot/don't shoot" scenarios, additional police training should be considered.

Value of Total Incident Training

Most shooting situations escalate from some other type of call for service, but many departments have little total incident training. Except for initial firearms training of officers, firearms/weapons training in isolation can be counterproductive for police. Police training officers go to the range to shoot. They go to shoot/don't shoot training to shoot. For instance, our original "edge weapons" training which included learning the "21-foot rule" left me feeling as though I must shoot or be stabbed. If officers were never taught alternatives to shooting, you can see why they would feel that shooting was their only option.

Total incident training can assist the officer to assess the totality of the situation and provide alternate methods to de-escalate a perceived or actual threat. Rather than merely relying on instinct, officers are trained to think for themselves. Officers should ask themselves, "What is really going on here?"

I can only remember attending one police training scenario when we were not supposed to shoot. The suspicious call involved a kid standing with his back to the officer who does not respond to commands. He puts his hands in his pocket and finally turns around quickly, pulling something out of his pocket. Fearing a weapon, officers often shoot (also because they're at shooting training). In his hand is a card that says, "I am a deaf-mute."

Progressive police departments that include total incident training as part of their firearms training often find themselves in a better light after an officer-involved shooting. Which sounds better? "The officer was legally authorized to use deadly force" or "The officer assessed the totality of the situation and was forced to shoot the aggressor to stop the deadly action."

Police officers are often required to make the decision to

shoot in a split second. But as the knife incident above illustrates, situations do arise when an officer has time to consider other methods to resolve the conflict.

During officer training, there are only brief discussions about the changing dynamics of a combat situation. In shoot/don't shoot training, discussions involve whether officers have the legal authority to shoot. Once it is deemed they have a green light to shoot, alternatives are seldom, if ever, discussed. Training programs must address alternatives to assist the officer during the decision-making process about whether or not to use deadly force.

Making such a decision involves in-depth training and role-playing scenarios. Police officers are paid to risk their lives, but they certainly should not be expected to take a bullet due to slow decision making. This article does not suggest that a police officer should always consider a less-than-lethal alternative in every situation.

In the knife situation outlined above, the officer would have been justified shooting the youngster. Hold on! The police officer admitted the kid wasn't trying to stab him; he was attempting to use the butcher knife on the other kid. That's true, but the officer has the responsibility to protect all lives. That includes the officer's life and the other kid's life, as well as the aggressor's life.

Using Real-Life Training Scenarios

Firearms training should include real-life situations such as the knife and deaf-mute incidents mentioned above like this to promote discussions. Officers should place themselves in these situations and think about alternative ways to resolve the threat, but only if the incident allows for ample time. Input by the firearms training staff is imperative, but officers should be encouraged to brainstorm alternative methods and actions.

Any police department, no matter how small, should have no problem identifying real-life scenarios for training and discussion. Caution should be taken, however, to avoid incidents under investigation or review. Additionally, no officer should be ridiculed or otherwise made to feel he acted improperly after using deadly force. Only the officer(s) involved in the incident were there and as long as their actions were deemed legal, their decision as to how to handle it should never be questioned by their peers.

In summary, if a police officer is justified in using deadly force, the officer should never risk his life or jeopardize the safety of others by being reluctant to do so. However, if time permits during an incident, it is important that officers seek out alternative less-than-lethal methods to help preserve life.

A word about transparency is in order. We constantly hear the public critique police shootings with such ridiculous statements such as: "The cop didn't have to kill him. He could have just shot him in the leg or something." Or: "He was only a boy, he had his whole life ahead of him." News flash! Police officers are not trained to kill people. They are trained to neutralize a person's aggressive acts. Officers are trained to shoot at the torso, the large body mass, because it's the easiest part of the body to hit. This isn't target shooting, folks.

Therefore, in addition to training police personnel, police departments would do well to train their communities. A "Citizen's Police Academy" is, in my opinion, one of the best ways of teaching the public why police officers respond the way they do. I have spoken with many citizens who have completed training offered by police departments and every one was positively enlightened by what he or she learned.

There are two basic schools of thought concerning firearms police training and police-involved shootings. The primary goal of police administrations is to prevent and/or reduce liability. The officers' major goal is to protect the citizens they serve and to come home to their families safe each night. Police departments do not have to take sides or settle for one goal or the other. Both can be achieved with appropriate and consistent police training.

Organizations to Contact

The editors have compiled the following list of organizations concerned with the issues debated in this book. The descriptions are derived from materials provided by the organizations. All have publications or information available for interested readers. This list was compiled on the date of publication of the present volume; the information provided here may change. Be aware that many organizations take several weeks or longer to respond to inquiries, so allow as much time as possible.

+Acumen
(212) 566-8821
email: courses@plusacumen.org
website: www.plusacumen.org

+Acumen is an organization that offers free and low-price courses for people who are interested in making social changes. The organization has various partners—including the US Department of Labor—who assist in helping the organization grow. All in all, +Acumen also has a network of 300,000 students within 190 different countries who are helping to make social change across the globe.

American Civil Liberties Union
125 Broad Street, 18th Floor,
New York, NY 10004
(212) 549-2500
website: www.aclu.org

The American Civil Liberties Union (ACLU) is an organization that has worked to defend the people's constitutional rights for nearly 100 years. Made up of more than 1.6 million members, the ACLU is also America's largest public interest law firm, with all 50 states being represented. The ACLU is nonprofit and non-partisan and is headquartered in New York City.

Black Lives Matter
website: www.blacklivesmatter.com

Black Lives Matter is an online forum dedicated to building a community of people to help fight against anti-black racism and to develop the necessary connections needed to end social injustice. The movement was formed in 2013 by Patrisse Cullors, Opal Tometi, and Alicia Garza and has since expanded into a national movement with chapters across the country. Various BLM chapters have been covered by the media in the last few years due to high-profile police shootings.

Black Youth Project 100
PO Box 9031
Chicago, IL 60609
(773) 940-1800
email: info@byp100.org
website: www.byp100.org

The Black Youth Project is an activist member-based organization of African American men and women between the ages of eighteen and thirty-five. The mission of the organization is to train young black individuals on social justice in hopes of ending criminalization as well as police brutality and racial profiling. BYP100 members are asked to contribute $10 per month to the organization and dedicate a minimum of three hours per week to the organization's matters.

Center for American Progress
1333 H Street
Washington, DC 20005
(202) 682-1611
website: www.americanprogressaction.org

Founded in 2003, the Center for American Progress Action Fund is a nonprofit organization that is dedicated to improving the lives of Americans through forward-thinking ideas, strong leadership, and action.

International Association of Chiefs of Police
44 Canal Center Plaza Suite 200
Alexandria, VA 22314
(703) 836-6767
website: www.theiacp.org

International Association of Chiefs of Police is an organization dedicated to advancing law enforcement through advocacy and education programs. While the organization does many things, one of its main focuses is on the training of police officers. The IACP is made up of 30,000 members throughout 146 countries around the world.

International Law Enforcement Educators and Trainers Association
8150 White Oak Avenue
Munster, IN 46321
(262) 767-1406
email: info@ileeta.org
website: www.ileeta.org

International Law Enforcement Educators and Trainers Association is an organization dedicated to the training of police officers and various arms of law enforcement. One of ILEETA's main focuses is to ensure the safety and security of citizens, while improving the understanding and communication within the communities officers serve. ILEETA holds an annual conference that more than 800 members attend.

National Association Against Police Brutality
PO Box 64170
Washington, DC 20019
(202) 749-9775
email: info@naapb.org
website: www.naapb.org

The National Association Against Police Brutality was founded by Jonathan Newton, a law student who was a former police officer, as part of community service requirements for his degree. Formed in December 2014, the entity's goals include educating citizens on their civil rights as well as assisting citizens in legal aid against those who were victimized by the police, among other things. Since its creation, the organization's website states that it's received more than eight hundred calls regarding people seeking assistance following an encounter with an unprofessional officer of the law.

National Police Accountability Project
499 7th Avenue, Suite 12N
New York, NY 10018
(212) 630-9939
email: assistant.npap@nlg.org
website: www.nlg-npap.org

The National Police Accountability Project is a nonprofit organization dedicated to protecting the civil rights of people who have encounters with law enforcement. A central mission of the NPAP is to develop accountability of police officers when violating constitutional laws. The NPAP is a project of the National Lawyers Guild, which was founded in 1937 as an alternative to the American Bar Association.

The Trace
email: info@thetrace.org
website: www.thetrace.org

The Trace is a nonprofit news organization that serves to educate its readership on gun usage and violence in America. The Trace, in partnership with a company called Slate, has built an interactive map that shows the locations of nearly 40,000 gun-related incidents, also providing information and details on the incidents. The organization not only reports on news, but also reports on potential fixes for the gun epidemic that the United States currently faces.

Bibliography

Books

Alison Behnke. *Racial Profiling: Everyday Inequality*. Minneapolis, MN: Lerner Publishing Group, 2017.

Stephen Egharevba. *Police Brutality, Racial Profiling, and Discrimination in the Criminal Justice System*. Hershey, PA: IGI-Global, 2016.

Thomas Fensch. *The Sordid Hypocrisy of to Protect and to Serve: Police Brutality, Corruption and Oppression in America*. New Century Books, 2015.

Skolnick Fyfe. *Above the Law: Police and the Excessive Use of Force*. New York, NY: Free Press, 2010.

Corinne Grinapol. *Racial Profiling and Discrimination: Your Legal Rights*. New York, NY: Rosen Young Adult, 2015.

Maria R. Haberfeld. *Critical Issues in Police Training*. Edition 1. Saddle River, NJ: Prentice Hall, 2002.

Las Vegas Review Journal. *Deadly Force: When Las Vegas Police Shoot, and Kill*. Las Vegas, NV: Stephens Press, LLC, 2011.

Alana Lentin. *Racism and Ethnic Discrimination*. New York, NY: Rosen Publishing Group, 2011.

Autumn Libal. *Discrimination & Prejudice*. Broomall, PA: National Highlights Inc., 2014.

James P. Mcelvain. *Police Shootings and Citizen Behavior*. El Paso, TX: LFB Scholarly Publishing LLC, 2008.

Seumas Miller. *Shooting to Kill: The Ethics of Police and Military Use of Lethal Force*. New York, NY: Oxford University Press, 2016.

Cliff Roberson. *Police Misconduct: A Global Perspective*. Boca Raton, FL: CRC Press, 2017.

Michael Ruth. *Police Brutality*. New York, NY: Greenhaven Publishing, 2016.

Bill Stonehem. *Police Shootings on the Rise in the United States*. Self-Published, 2016.

US Department of Justice. *The Role of Police Psychology in Controlling Excessive Force*. Washington, DC: U.S. Department of Justice, 2016.

Periodicals and Internet Sources

Michael A. Cohen. "Dallas Police Department Leads the Way in Se-escalation," *Boston Globe*, July 9, 2016, https://www.bostonglobe.com/opinion/2016/07/08/dallas-police-department-leads-way-escalation/pxvSK7SpFx86m3mV3UuJbI/story.html.

Camila Domonoske. "Shots in the Back, Children Tasered: DOJ Details Excessive Force by Chicago Police," NPR, January 13, 2017, http://www.npr.org/sections/thetwo-way/2017/01/13/509665735/shots-in-the-back-children-tasered-doj-details-excessive-force-by-chicago-police.

Jason Hanna and Madison Park. "Chicago Police Use Excessive Force, DOJ Finds," CNN, January 13, 2017, http://www.cnn.com/2017/01/13/us/chicago-police-federal-investigation/index.html.

Tom Jackman. "De-escalation Training to Reduce Police Shootings Facing Mixed Reviews at Launch," *Washington Post*, October 15, 2016, https://www.washingtonpost.com/local/public-safety/de-escalation-training-to-reduce-police-shootings-facing-mixed-reviews-at-launch/2016/10/14/d6d96c74-9159-11e6-9c85-ac42097b8cc0_story.html?utm_term=.14b0b4056567.

Kimberly Kindy. "New Style of Police Training Aims to Produce 'Guardians,' not 'Warriors,'" *Washington Post*, December 10, 2015, http://www.washingtonpost.com/sf/

investigative/2015/12/10/new-style-of-police-training-aims-to-produce-guardians-not-warriors/?utm_term=.b8a9e2475e31.

Wesley Lowery. "Police Chiefs Consider Dramatic Reforms to Officer Tactics, Training to Prevent So Many Shootings," *Washington Post*, January 29, 2016, https://www.washingtonpost.com/news/post-nation/wp/2016/01/29/police-chiefs-consider-dramatic-reforms-to-officer-tactics-training-to-prevent-so-many-shootings/?utm_term=.40867e3b715b.

Barbara Reynolds. "I Was a Civil Rights Activist in the 1960s. But It's Hard for Me to Get Behind Black Lives Matter," *Washington Post*, August 24, 2015, https://www.washingtonpost.com/posteverything/wp/2015/08/24/i-was-a-civil-rights-activist-in-the-1960s-but-its-hard-for-me-to-get-behind-black-lives-matter/?utm_term=.5875e1f2c49a.

Brad W. Smith and Malcolm D. Holmes. "Police Use of Excessive Force in Minority Communities: A Test of the Minority Threat, Place, and Community Accountability Hypotheses," Oxford Academic, July 24, 2014, https://academic.oup.com/socpro/article-abstract/61/1/83/1626052

Katherine Spillar. "How More Female Police Officers Would Help Stop Police Brutality," *Washington Post*, July 2, 2015, https://www.washingtonpost.com/posteverything/wp/2015/07/02/how-more-female-police-officers-would-help-stop-police-brutality/?utm_term=.492d1d3e171c.

Seth Stoughton. "How Police Training Contributes to Avoidable Deaths," *Atlantic*, December 12, 2014, https://www.theatlantic.com/national/archive/2014/12/police-gun-shooting-training-ferguson/383681/.

Phillip Swarts. "Police Need Better Training and Community Relations, Presidential Task Force Is Told," *Washington Times*, January 13, 2015, http://www.washingtontimes.com/

news/2015/jan/13/police-brutality-solutions-are-training-community-/.

Annie Sweeney. "Police 'De-escalation' Training — How It Could Help Chicago," *Chicago Tribune*, March 25, 2016, http://www.chicagotribune.com/news/ct-police-training-las-vegas-chicago-met-20160324-story.html.

Juleyka Lantigua-Williams. "How Much Can Better Training Do to Improve Policing?" *Atlantic*, July 13, 2016, https://www.theatlantic.com/politics/archive/2016/07/police-training/490556/.

Timothy Williams. "Long Taught to Use Force, Police Warily Learn to De-escalate," *New York Times*, June 27, 2015, https://www.nytimes.com/2015/06/28/us/long-taught-to-use-force-police-warily-learn-to-de-escalate.html.

Holly Yan. "States Require More Training Time to Become a Barber than a Police Officer," CNN, September 28, 2016, http://www.cnn.com/2016/09/28/us/jobs-training-police-trnd/index.html.

Index

Obama, Barack, 49–50, 71,
106, 114, 115, 129, 131,
133, 140, 147
"Operation Ghetto Storm,"
108–109

P

Palomino, Joaquin, 123–127
Pastore, Nick, 113
perjury, 82, 83, 88
Philadelphia Police
Department, 21, 129, 145,
149
Piquero, Alex R., 22
police
danger of police power,
144–150
discrimination toward,
47–53, 54–56, 73
distrust of, 18–19, 36, 47, 74,
88, 92, 115, 129, 131,
143
effect of violence/fear on,
61–65, 85, 142–143
interactions with, 114–118
killing of, 19, 52, 62, 64,
140–141
lack of punishment for
deaths caused by,
100–103, 111, 146
lying/perjury by, 82–88
militarization of, 90–91, 98,
105, 112–113, 115, 131,
142, 147

reforms needed, 80–81, 92,
129–131, 140–143,
145–149
poor, death by police of the,
104–107
Porter, William, 101
Portland Police Bureau,
decrease in use of force,
119–122
Powell, Kajieme, 40, 45, 135
prisons, deaths in, 116

Q

qualified immunity, 79–80

R

racial profiling, 23–24, 109–
110, 117, 132, 147
racism, 18, 23, 29, 32, 38, 40,
47, 50, 51, 63, 75, 98, 105,
108–109, 110, 111, 113
Ramsey, Charles, 129, 131–
132, 149
Razey, Bruce, 156–160
Reagan, Ronald, 112
Reese, Mike, 119, 120–121
Reisig, Michael D., 24–25
Reynolds, Lavish, 61
Rice, Tamir, 17, 28, 32, 41, 74
Ringgenberg, Mark, 103
Rosenfeld, Steven, 32–39
Rowe, Donyale, 97
Rudovsky, David, 144–150